LITTLE BOOK OF
BRITISH
COMEDY GREATS

LITTLE BOOK OF
BRITISH
COMEDY GREATS

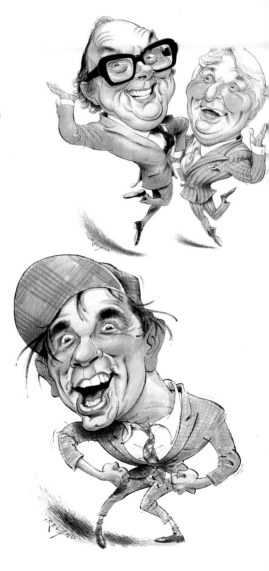

First published in the UK in 2012

© Demand Media Limited 2012

www.demand-media.co.uk

Printed and bound in China

ISBN 978-1-909217-07-2

Contents

Rowan Atkinson

Rowan Sebastian Atkinson was born on 6th January 1955 in Consett, County Durham.

Rowan Atkinson is arguably one of the greatest living and performing comedians of the twenty-first century. Atkinson's humour is to the British hilarious; he has something for everyone.

First bursting onto the British comedy scene in 1978 on BBC Radio 3, he co-wrote (with his university friend Richard Curtis) and starred in a series of satirical comedy shows called The Atkinson People. The series was produced by Griff Rhys Jones.

Since then he has become famous for numerous collaborations, roles and characters, most notably Not the Nine O'Clock News, Blackadder (all four series), Mr Bean, The Thin Blue Line, and Jonny English.

Atkinson has received two 'Best Light Entertainment Performance' BAFTA Awards during his career to date: in 1981 for Not the Nine O'Clock News, and in 1990 for Blackadder Goes Forth.

Film work has also played an important part in Atkinson's career and he has appeared in numerous box office hits including, the 'unofficial' James Bond film Never Say Never Again, The Tall Guy, Roald Dahl's The Witches, Four Weddings and a Funeral, and Love Actually, to name a few.

In terms of his comic style, Atkinson is a master of both verbal and visual comedy. Being forced to manage a stutter all of his life, he has successfully turned his technique of coping with it into one of the most amusing and characteristic features of his comedy.

Starred in:
Not the Nine
O'Clock News
Blackadder
Mr Bean
The Thin Blue Line
Jonny English

Awards:
Two BAFTA Light
Entertainment
Awards

"Atkinson is a master of both *verbal* and *visual* comedy"

A particularly memorable example of this mastery is his way of verbally over pronouncing the letter 'b' for Bob in the episode 'Bells' of Blackadder II.

The character of Mr. Bean is the epitome of his physical comic acting skills. Unlike the majority of Atkinson's other famous comic roles (whose characters require a combination of comic verbal and body language), Mr Bean relies solely on the physical performance to create hilarity. Sometimes called 'the man with the rubber face', he uses his extraordinary skill for facial expression to comic effect like no other.

Atkinson is an extremely versatile comic actor and, over his career, he has moved seamlessly from radio to television, and film to theatre. His skills as a satiric screenwriter are also well known and celebrated. He was a major contributor to the Not the Nine O'Clock News sketches, wrote the original The Black Adder with Richard Curtis, as well as creating the character of Mr Bean.

Atkinson's comic style is totally unique and he has now become an iconic British comedy figure. The entire Blackadder series is regarded as one of the greatest comedy creations of all time.

Atkinson's visual comedy playing Mr Bean is captured here brilliantly

LEFT Atkinson in The Thin Blue Line

Ronnie
Barker

Ronald William George Barker, OBE
was born on 25th September 1929 in Bedford, Bedfordshire. He died at the age of 76 on 3rd October 2005.

A comic genius who has entertained families throughout the nation for generations, Ronnie Barker's humour and talent has been sorely missed from our screens since his death in 2005.

Most notably known and loved for his roles in The Frost Report, The Two Ronnies, Porridge, and Open All Hours, Barker is one of Britain's most loved and respected comedians of the twentieth century. As well as being a talented comic actor, Barker was also a respected comic writer and critic, under the pseudonym Gerald Wiley.

Known predominantly as a talented comic actor, as opposed to a comedian, Barker performed every comic role with precision and sincerity; he believed wholeheartedly in what he did. As a comic writer he was concerned with precision and timing, as well as careful choice of language. Barker was not one for crude or obscene jokes, but preferred to use language to create risqué innuendos for comic effect.

Barker's comic career began on the theatrical stage before his success in this field enabled him to move to radio. Perhaps his most memorable performances from this early stage in his career were in The Navy Lark. Barker played several characters in the radio sitcom that ran from 1959 to 1977, performing in around 300 episodes.

The turning point in his career came in 1966, with the satirical sketch series The Frost Report, firmly establishing himself in the British comedy world.

"Barker is one of Britain's most loved and respected comedians of the twentieth century"

Starred in:
The Frost Report
The Two Ronnies
Porridge
Open All Hours

Awards:
OBE
Four BAFTA Light Entertainment Awards

IRELAND

"A *comic genius* who has *entertained* families throughout the nation for *generations*"

Performing alongside David Frost, John Cleese and his future comic partner Ronnie Corbett, the series became the nucleus for their later sketch show, The Two Ronnies.

Prior to The Two Ronnies, Barker had his own show, The Ronnie Barker Playhouse and David Frost also moved to ITV to present Frost on Sunday. As Barker and Corbett became a frequently featured comedy pair on Frost's programme, so Barker started writing sketches (which continued throughout his career) under his pseudonym, Gerald Wiley.

With the move to the BBC and The Two Ronnies under way, it became arguably Barker's most successful collaboration. With his sidekick Ronnie Corbett, the pair made men, women and children alike fall off their living room chairs laughing with their comedy sketch show from 1971 to 1986.

The Two Ronnies was running successfully, which gave Barker the opportunity to get involved in another sitcom on his own. Starring as the prisoner Fletcher, Porridge (originally called Prisoner and Escort) ran with enormous success from 1974 to 1977. It is now widely regarded as one of British comedy sitcom's classics.

Open All Hours was at first, quite frankly, a flop. It was first aired on BBC 2 in 1976 and, given the low ratings the sitcom received, only one series was broadcast. That was until the series was repeated on BBC 1. Following its huge success second time around, the BBC requested a second series of the comedy in 1981; two further series followed as its ratings continued to soar.

Barker received an OBE in 1978 as well as receiving four BAFTA 'Best Light Entertainment Performance' Awards during his career.

RIGHT Barker as one of his classic characters, 'Fletcher' in Porridge

Stanley Baxter

Stanley Baxter
was born on
24th May 1926
in Glasgow,
Scotland

Stanley Baxter's self-titled comedy series were an unmissable and endearing part of television entertainment throughout the 1960s, 70s and 80s.

His elasticated face and accentuated pronunciation tickled the nation's funny bone and his impressions of famous people, particularly the Queen (referred to as 'the Duchess of Brenda') became part of our comedy diet.

His shows were always manically over the top with lavish sets and technically demanding set pieces and in his pomp he won many BAFTA Light Entertainment Awards.

Many of today's celebrity comedians pay homage to the Scottish comedian while, sadly, younger audiences have little idea of who he was and the influence his shows had on the current-day heroes.

The son of an insurance manager, Baxter was born in Glasgow and nurtured his career on the stage and radio before turning his talents to television. The Stanley Baxter Show ran between 1963 and 1971 on BBC One; the Stanley Baxter Picture Show from 1972 to 1975 on ITV; and the six-part Stanley Baxter Series on LWT in 1981. Some eight one-hour TV specials were made by LWT and the BBC between 1973 and 1986.

Whilst his television specials were at one time as popular as the likes of Morecambe & Wise, perhaps his best-known series of sketches was Parliamo Glasgow, a pastiche of the BBC's first venture into language programmes.

One of his most memorable scenes saw him asking a market trader, "Zarra

"His shows were always manically over the top with lavish sets and technically demanding set pieces"

marra onna barra, Clara?" which he then gruffly translated as "Is that a marrow on your barrow, Clara?"

He guest starred in other television shows – including an episode of The Goodies – as well as a number of children's shows and in Bing Crosby's final Christmas special taped just before his death in 1977, where he played multiple roles including Charles Dickens and the ghost of Bob Hope.

That he faded from public view (and his hour-long television show axed) was due in part to his act being firmly based in vaudeville and his style being that of a music hall entertainer. It was good, even 'great' British comedy, it was just that it was of its time.

Starred in:
The Stanley Baxter Show
The Stanley Baxter Picture Show
Stanley Baxter Series
Parliamo Glasgow

Awards:
BAFTA Light Entertainment Awards

"Stanley Baxter's self-titled comedy series were an unmissable and endearing part of television entertainment"

Rodney Bewes

Rodney Bewes was born on 27th November 1937 in Bingley, West Riding of Yorkshire.

Known as a chubby-cheeked comedy actor, Rodney Bewes is much admired and remembered most notably for his role as Bob Ferris in the television sitcom The Likely Lads. He is also a talented and recognised screenwriter and writer.

Bewes' acting career started when he was young, acting in BBC plays when he was 12 and then attending the preparatory school of the Royal Academy of Dramatic Arts (RADA), prior to studying at the main Academy. His early career started on the stage in London alongside the likes of Richard Briers and Brian Murphy.

Before Bewes was cast for the role that really changed his fortune, he appeared in Dixon of Dock Green in 1962, Z-Cars in 1963, and (with his good friend Tom Courtenay) in the 1963 classic film Billy Liar.

The success of The Likely Lads turned Bewes (and his co-star James Bolam) into household names. An estimated 27 million people watched the series, that's almost half the country's population! It initially ran as a television sitcom from 1964 to 1966.

The second series, Whatever Happened To The Likely Lads, first broadcast in 1973 was even more popular than their first. Bewes had become firmly established as part of many British households' comedy furniture. In 1976 a feature film called The Likely Lads followed, but it was not the box office hit that some thought it would be.

Unfortunately Bewes and Bolam, once as good friends off the set as on it, fell out some 30 or so years ago. The on-

"The *Likely Lads* turned Bewes into
a *household name. An estimated*
27 million people watched the series"

going feud between them is one of the longest in show business, which is all strangely ironic considering their series and subsequent success was totally based around an enduring friendship!

Bewes' comedy career was in full swing from the mid-1960s for a decade. In between the two Likely Lads series, he also performed in several other shows including Man in a Suitcase and The Basil Brush Show. Between 1969 and 1972, he also co-wrote and starred in his own sitcom, Dear Mother … Love Albert.

Although he is most fondly remembered as a television sitcom actor, Bewes also appeared in a number of films during the 1960s and 1970s, including Alice's Adventures in Wonderland in 1972, in which he played the Knave of Hearts, The Three Musketeers in 1973,

and The Spaceman and King Arthur in 1979.

Bewes is admittedly still very proud of his comedy roles, particularly as Bob Ferris in The Likely Lads. Since the end of that era, however, Bewes' acting career has been a little inconsistent, although his stage work has proved more popular, particularly his one-man versions of Three Men in a Boat and Diary of a Nobody. Bewes now concentrates on touring the United Kingdom with both of his shows.

Starred in:
The Likely Lads
Whatever
Happened To The
Likely Lads
Dixon of Dock
Green
Z-Cars
Dear Mother

"He is also a **talented** and
recognised **screenwriter**
and **writer**"

Wilfrid Brambell

**Henry Wilfrid
Brambell** was
born on 22nd
March 1912 in
Dublin, Ireland.
He died at the age
of 72 on 18th
January
1985.

Even though Wilfrid Brambell was born in Dublin, his success and impact on British comedy and British audiences has been significant, and he therefore undoubtedly deserves a place here amongst the British Comedy Greats.

Brambell is most famously known and loved for his role as Albert Steptoe in Steptoe and Son, and this was the role that endeared him to people nationwide. He had, however, had a varied and prolific acting career for many years before this.

Brambell became interested in acting from a young age, and started when still a child in Dublin first entertaining injured soldiers during World War I, before moving to the Abbey Theatre. Turning professional, he then moved to the Gate Theatre. His love of theatre continued throughout his career and he was cast in many plays and even musicals.

His television career began in the 1950s

"Acting for over half a century,
*Brambell's **extremely versatile***
acting talents have been celebrated"

and he appeared in several BBC television dramas including The Quatermass Experiment in 1953, Nineteen Eighty-Four in 1954, and Quatermass II in 1955. Even though he was only in his forties, the characters he played in these productions initiated his reputation for playing old men.

It was his character as a lonely grandfather in ITV's Television Playhouse play No Fixed Abode that led him to his most famous role, that of Albert Steptoe in Steptoe and Son.

Written by Ray Galton and Alan Simpson, and playing alongside Harry Corbett as his son Harold, the comedy sitcom's first full series ran from 1962 to 1965 and was very successful. A second series was then broadcast from 1970 to 1974 by which time Alfred Steptoe had become one of the nation's most high-profile comedy characters.

Even though Brambell's affinity to playing old men was something that he couldn't get away from, it did lead to other roles, one of the most notable being Paul McCartney's fictional grandfather in The Beatles 1964 film A Hard Day's Night.

Ironically Brambell will always be associated with his character Alfred in Steptoe and Son, even though off the screen he was a very smartly dressed, well-spoken gentleman.

Acting for over half a century, Brambell's extremely versatile acting talents have been celebrated, and he could be cast in anything from Shakespeare to Orwell and more than do it justice. Unfortunately his latter life was affected by alcohol; it was almost as if he couldn't shake off the association and image of him as 'a dirty old man' in Steptoe and Son.

Starred in:
No Fixed Abode
Steptoe and Son
A Hard Day's
Night

LEFT Wilfred Bramble & Harry H Corbett as the legendary Steptoe and Son

Richard
Briers

Richard David Briers, CBE
was born on 14th January 1934 in Raynes Park, Surrey.

Undoubtedly one of our most talented comedy actors, Richard Briers is a household name and a professional master of all acting mediums in the theatre, on the radio, and in television and film.

His talent throughout his career, which began in the late 1950s, has earned him great accolade and recognition: Briers was awarded an OBE in 1989 and a CBE in 2003.

As with many a budding acting star, Briers started out on the stage, studying at RADA from 1954 to 1956. He then won a scholarship with the Liverpool Repertory Company. From there he moved to perform at the Belgrade Theatre in Coventry before he landed his first acting job in the West End.

As a comedy television actor Briers was spotted in 1962 by Frank Muir and Denis Norden, who gave him his first ever leading role in the BBC's legal comedy series Brothers in Law. His first taste of real stardom came, however, when he was cast alongside Prunella Scales as George Starling in the black-and-white comedy Marriage Lines that ran from 1963 to 1966. Although this was the series that catapulted Briers permanently into the lives and hearts of British audiences nationwide, he had many other comic roles prior to this, including The Morecambe & Wise Show.

Briers' major career break came in 1975 when he was cast as Tom Good in The Good Life. Written by John Esmonde and Bob Larbey the television comedy series was hugely successful and ran until 1978. In 1984 the same writers then cast him as Martin Bryce in Ever Decreasing Circles. Another highly successful BBC sitcom that was perhaps darker in comedy style, it ran for 27 episodes over four years.

Apart from being chosen for a lead role in the third Esmonde and Larbey collaboration in the 1995 sitcom Down to Earth, Briers played many other roles throughout the 1980s and 1990s including Tales of the Unexpected, Mr Bean, and If You See God, Tell Him.

Although very well known for his comedy roles, Briers' acting career spans numerous other entertainment genres from theatre to radio, as well as films. His expressive and 'easy-to-listen-to voice' has also won him numerous advertising jobs, and famous children's animation roles including Roobarb, Watership Down, Jackanory and two episodes of the ITV television series The Wind in the Willows, where he was the voice of Rat.

Briers' association with Kenneth Branagh has enhanced his career in film and he has appeared in Henry V and Peter's Friends in 1992, Much Ado About Nothing in 1993, Mary Shelley's Frankenstein in 1994, Hamlet in 1996, and Love's Labours Lost in 2000.

Briers has also played many less comic and more dramatic television roles during his career which include being cast in series such as Dixon of Dock Green, Lovejoy, Inspector Morse, New Tricks, and Monarch of the Glen.

Starred in:
Marriage Line
The Good Life
Ever Decreasing
Circles
Down to Earth

Peter Butterworth

Peter William Shorrocks Butterworth was born on 4th February 1919 in Stockport, Cheshire. He died at the age of 59 on 16th January 1979

One of our most endearing and talented British comedy actors, Peter Butterworth had an extremely successful acting career for over 30 years before his untimely death from a heart attack at the age of 59.

Although his show business experience was vast and varied, he is perhaps most commonly associated with his appearances in many of the 'Carry On' films.

Time spent in the World War II prison camp Stalag Luft III was where it all began. As well as giving him the opportunity for his first attempt at performing in front of an audience, he also made significant connections and friends whilst there. He became close friends with English screenwriter Talbot Rothwell, and other future actors in the same camp included Rupert Davies, Stratford Johns and John Casson.

Performing in pantomimes in the U.K. was the first thing that got him seriously noticed by those in the entertainment industry. 1948 was the year of his first film appearance in William Come to Town, by British film director Val Guest. The two became good friends and over their respective careers would work together on seven subsequent films. During his career Butterworth also worked alongside such film stars as David Niven, Sean Connery, Audrey Hepburn and Richard Harris.

The first acting role that brought Butterworth to the attention of the British people was the role of chauffeur Lockitt, which he played in the Terry-Thomas television sketch series How Do You View? During the 1950s he

"Peter Butterworth had an extremely successful acting career for over 30 years"

also presented children's television programmes including Butterworth Time and Whirligig.

Butterworth's first 'Carry On' appearance was in the 1965 film Carry On Cowboy. He quickly became one of the regular 'Carry On' team and was in 16 of the films in total. Perhaps the two most memorable and well-known were Carry On Up The Khyber and Carry On Camping.

Butterworth was also part of the two Christmas specials made, and the 1975 television series. With Barbara Windsor, Sid James and Kenneth Connor, he was also part of the 'Carry On' West End stage production that ended up touring the country.

Following the final 'Carry On' film, Carry On Emmanuelle in 1978, Butterworth was cast with smaller parts in more serious films including The First Great Train Robbery. His love for pantomime never waned, and whilst performing in Aladdin at the Coventry Theatre in 1979 it unfortunately became the very last role he played. Butterworth had a heart attack after the performance on 16th January.

Starred in:
How Do You View
The 'Carry On'
Series
And many
West End shows

"One of our most endearing and talented British comedy actors"

Frank Carson

Hugh Francis Carson, KSG was born on 6th November 1926 in Belfast, Northern Ireland. He died at the age of 85 on 22nd February 2012.

A much loved and respected comedian, Northern Ireland-born Frank Carson made many people laugh, and he also helped as many people through his dedication and passion for charity work.

Having sadly passed away in February 2012, as expressed by one of his nephews, '... he has passed on to join the great comedy legends of our generation'.

Before Carson found his career anchor in comedy, he had a wonderful array of jobs, including being an electrician, a plasterer, and joining the Parachute Regiment.

Although Carson had already become a popular television personality in Ireland, the turning point in Carson's career came in the 1960s when he won Opportunity Knocks, ITV's television talent show three times. From there on in Carson's road to fame and wealth began.

Carson's career and popularity became firmly established in the 1970s (and in fact what he is perhaps most remembered for) with his appearances on the non-stop, stand-up comedy show The Comedians. He performed alongside many of his comic contemporaries including Tom O'Connor, Stan Boardman, and George Roper.

Carson became synonymous with two sayings in particular, 'It's a cracker!' and 'It's the way I tell 'em!' After the success of The Comedians, he continued to appear regularly on television comedy shows, as well as performing on stage as an entertainer. New programmes in a similar vein to The Comedians were also broadcast, such as The Wheeltappers

*Carson became synonymous
with two sayings in particular,*
'It's a cracker!' *and*
'It's the way I tell 'em!'

Highlights:
won Opportunity
Knocks three
times
The non-stop
The Wheeltappers
and Shunters
Social Club
Tiswas

Awards:
Knighthood

and Shunters Social Club, in which Carson also played a part.

Making regular appearances on the Saturday morning children's series Tiswas, which ran from 1975 to 1982, Carson had pretty much covered every string to his comedy-career bow. Even later on in his life he continued to perform live, in pantomime and for cabaret.

In addition to his talent for and dedication to comedy, Carson also managed to fit in being Mayor of Balbriggan near Dublin, he became a member of the UK Independence Party and took his politics seriously for a while. Charity work was also extremely important to him, which was acknowledged when the Vatican and Pope John Paul II honoured him, and he became a Knight of St. Gregory.

Charlie Chaplin

Sir Charles Spencer Chaplin, KBE was born on 16th April 1889 in Walworth, London, and died on 25th December 1977.

Few British Comedy Greats can claim to be world stars, but Charlie Chaplin's little tramp was an international icon recognisable from Tintagel to Timbuktu.

He has also stood the test of time, as the tramp character was created for the silent movies, first appearing in the Keystone comedy Kid Auto Races at Venice in 1914 and is still instantly identifiable today.

But he was very much more than just a comic actor, as he was also an award-winning film producer, director and composer. He even had a number one hit with Petula Clark's rendition of his composition This is My Song.

At the height of his fame, before the end of World War I, he was the most famous film star in the world, or should we say his character, the tramp, was the most famous film star in the world.

Chaplin recalled how he created him: 'I wanted everything to be a contradiction: the pants baggy, the coat tight, the hat small and the shoes large. I was undecided whether to look old or young, but remembering Sennett had expected me to be a much older man, I added a small moustache which, I reasoned, would add age without hiding my expression. I had no idea of the character. But the moment I was dressed, the clothes and the makeup made me feel the person he was. I began to know him, and by the time I walked on stage he was fully born.'

The tramp was closely identified with the silent era and when the sound era began in the late 1920s Chaplin refused to make a talkie featuring the character.

Mary Pickford, Douglas Fairbanks and D. W. Griffith, he co-founded the film company United Artists in 1919.

Chaplin's working life in entertainment spanned more than 75 years but wasn't without controversy. He was identified with left-wing politics during the McCarthy era and he was ultimately forced to resettle in Europe from 1952.

Reviewer Martin Sieff summed up his career: 'Chaplin was not just 'big', he was gigantic. In 1915, he burst onto a war-torn world bringing it the gift of comedy, laughter and relief while it was tearing itself apart through World War I. Over the next 25 years, through the Great Depression and the rise of Adolf Hitler, he stayed on the job. ... It is doubtful any individual has ever given more entertainment, pleasure and relief to so many human beings when they needed it the most'.

Highlights:
'The tramp'
Kid Auto Races
This is My Song
Co-founded the film company United Artists

Awards:
Knighthood

He officially retired the character in the film Modern Times (1936) which fittingly ended with the tramp walking down an endless highway towards the horizon.

His career continued well into the era of the talkies, though his films decreased in frequency from the end of the 1920s. He was writing, producing and directing most of his films and with

Peter Cook

**Peter Edward
Cook** was born
on 17th November
1937 in Torquay,
Devon, and died
at the age of 57
on 9th January
1995.

Writer and comedian, Peter Cook, was regarded as one of the leading lights of the British satire boom of the 1960s and an anti-establishment figure.

Yet for his hardcore fans, he was simply an extraordinary comedian with a sense of timing and turn-of-phrase that could just as easily reduce his fellow performers to tears as his audience.

As sidekick to Dudley Moore, and as his dour E.L. Wisty character, he was on occasion deserving of Stephen Fry's accolade as 'the funniest man who ever drew breath'.

It was at Cambridge University that Cook performed and wrote comedy sketches as a member of the Cambridge Footlights Club, of which he became president in 1960. Whilst still at university, Cook wrote for Kenneth Williams, for whom he created an entire West End comedy revue called One Over the Eight, before finding prominence in his own right in a four-man group satirical stage show, Beyond the Fringe, with fellow students Jonathan Miller, Alan Bennett and Dudley Moore.

The show became a great success in London after being first performed at the Edinburgh Festival and included Cook impersonating the Prime Minister, Harold Macmillan; one of the first times satirical political mimicry had been attempted in live theatre.

In 1961 Cook opened The Establishment Club at Greek Street in Soho, showcasing fellow comedians in a nightclub setting, while his first regular television spot was on Granada Television's Braden Beat where he launched his most enduring character: the static and monotonal E.L. Wisty.

His partnership with Moore blossomed on Not Only... But Also where they created the inimitable 'Pete and Dud' partnership, a couple of down-and-outs who talked with pompous clarity about subjects which they knew nothing about.

Cook still maintained his rebelliousness and provided financial backing for the satirical magazine Private Eye, even supporting it through libel trials, and for a while the magazine was produced from the premises of The Establishment Club.

From the end of the 1960s, Cook's increasing alcoholism placed a strain on his personal and professional relationships. He and Moore fashioned sketches from Not Only... But Also with new material into the stage revue called Behind the Fridge, which toured Australia in 1972 before transferring to New York in 1973, re-titled as Good Evening.

Cook frequently appeared on and off stage the worse for drink. Nonetheless, the show proved very popular and it won Tony and Grammy Awards. When it finished, Moore stayed in the U.S. to pursue his burgeoning film career in Hollywood, effectively severing his partnership with Cook.

Prior to this professional parting, they had created the obscene rantings of 'Derek and Clive', to alleviate boredom during the Broadway run of Good Evening, and it caused an outrage when it was released in the U.K. on an LP.

Cook appeared in the first three fundraising galas staged by humourists John Cleese and Martin Lewis on behalf of Amnesty International, which went on to become The Secret Policeman's Balls. It wasn't until the third show in 1979, however, that the title was used.

In 1980 Cook moved to Hollywood, and partly spurred on by Moore's growing film star status, appeared as an uptight English butler to a wealthy American woman in a short-lived U.S. television sitcom The Two of Us. He also made cameo appearances in a couple of undistinguished films.

Throughout the decade he made sporadic appearances on pioneering television comedy in shows such as the first episode of Blackadder in 1983; and in The Comic Strip Presents' Mr Jolly Lives Next Door, in 1987, playing an assassin who covers the sound of his murders by playing Tom Jones records, but he never again reached the heights of his Pete & Dud years.

He could still occasionally show flashes of comic genius – as when he appeared on Clive Anderson Talks Back in 1993 as four characters: biscuit tester and alien abductee Norman House; football manager and motivational speaker Alan Latchley; judge Sir James Beauchamp; and rock legend Eric Daley. His lifelong heavy drinking, however, was always likely to catch up with him and he died from internal haemorrhaging at the start of 1995.

Highlights:
**One Over
the Eight
Beyond the Fringe
Pete and Dud
The Two of Us
Blackadder
Good Evening**

Awards:
**Good Evening
won Tony and
Grammy Awards**

John Cleese

and the
Monty Python Team

John Marwood Cleese was born on 27th October 1939 in Weston-super-Mare, Somerset.

Arguably one of the most talented and funny British actors born in the twentieth century, John Cleese is simply a comic genius at all levels, regardless of whether he is acting, writing or producing.

It all started at Cambridge University where he was reading Law, but spent a lot of time writing and performing for Footlights, the university's renowned drama club. The group went on to make such a serious impression with their revue entitled A Clump of Plinths at the Edinburgh Festival Fringe that, renamed Cambridge Circus, the Footlights revue ended up on the West End stage.

Cleese was effortlessly breaking into the British comedy world as a writer and performer. He contributed to many well-known shows at the time, but his real career breakthrough came with his writing and particularly performances on The Frost Report. Surrounded by many future great comic actors, it was during this period that the Pythons-to-be began collaborating.

The Monty Python team consisted

LEFT The Monty Python Team

of Cleese, Graham Chapman, Michael Palin, Terry Gilliam, Eric Idle and Terry Jones.

Cleese and the other members of the Monty Python team, have quite simply been unique and ingenious with their 'out there' sketches and films. The Monty Python humour is perhaps not everyone's cup of tea, although anyone with a sense of humour couldn't fail to find hilarity in the brilliant team! Ingeniously, and perhaps unintentionally, they created hours of entertainment that is absolutely timeless; Monty Python humour will always be funny, it will live forever.

JOHN CLEESE AND THE MONTY PYTHON TEAM

The sketch show Monty Python's Flying Circus ran for four seasons from October 1969 to December 1974. The success of their sketch show was the inspiration for their first film in 1971, And Now for Something Completely Different. This was followed by Monty Python and the Holy Grail in 1975, Life of Brian in 1979, Monty Python Live at the Hollywood Bowl in 1982, and The Meaning of Life in 1983.

Cleese's other famous roles include neurotic hotel manager Basil Fawlty in Fawlty Towers, which he co-wrote with his wife Connie in the mid-1970s. The series was so successful that it won three BAFTA Awards. Starring alongside Jamie Lee Curtis, Kevin Kline and former Python colleague Michael Palin, the film A Fish Called Wanda was nominated for an Academy Award for Cleese's screenplay.

Other popular films that Cleese starred in include Clockwise, and he also played the part of 'Nearly Headless Nick' in the first two Harry Potter films.

Cast in two Bond films, in The World Is Not Enough he was Q's nameless assistant, but due to the line 'If you're Q, does that make him R?', the name 'R' stuck! His second role was in Die Another Day as 'Q' that time.

Cleese has been a phenomenally successful comedy actor and writer since the early 1960s. He has been nominated for Academy, Golden Globe, BAFTA and Emmy Awards on numerous occasions for his acting and writing, and has won two BAFTA Awards and one Emmy Award to date.

John Cleese
Highlights:
Footlights Revue
The Frost Report
Monty Python
Fawlty Towers
A Fish Called
Wanda
Harry Potter films

Awards:
Two BAFTA
Awards
Emmy Award

Monty Python:
Three BAFTA
Awards

LEFT John Cleese in
Fawlty Towers

Billy
Connolly

William Connolly, Jr, CBE was born on 24th November 1942 in Anderston, Glasgow.

It may be an excusable misconception for those who have not closely followed Billy Connolly's career that he, albeit one of this country's greatest, is not just a brilliant stand-up comedian. Connolly is also a very successful presenter, actor and musician, and has also been voted the most influential comedian of all time.

Known affectionately by his nickname as 'The Big Yin', particularly in Scotland, Connolly began his adult life and career in the late 1960s as a folk singer, first in the band the Humblebums with Gerry Rafferty, then as a soloist. It was in fact the head of his record label, Nat Joseph from Transatlantic

Records, who suggested that he focused on becoming a comedian; these turned out to be very wise words indeed.

The BBC's prime time Saturday evening show Parkinson also proved to be a major turning point in Connolly's career as a comedian, and he even said himself that, 'That programme changed my entire life'. Not only did Connolly's first appearance and edgy humour make a big impact that first time, he became great friends with Michael Parkinson, and has been a guest on his show a record-breaking 15 further times. From there on in not only did his popularity become firmly established all over the U.K., it also spread to Canada, New Zealand and Australia. It seems that the Americans took longer to grasp the broad Scottish accent and his sense of humour; he didn't become known or popular in the U.S. until 1990!

As a stand-up comic Connolly is anything but politically correct, and he has very successfully managed to cause regular outrage with audiences throughout his career. His subject material is often not what one would discuss over dinner, and has included everything from blasphemy to haemorrhoids!

Releasing his work on albums has always played a big part in Connolly's life, right back to when he released his first in 1972 called Billy Connolly Live!, which was a combination of short monologues and comedic songs. Since then he has released 26 musical and comedic recordings, the last of which was The Man Live in London in 2010.

Music has remained an important part of Connolly's life albeit to a lesser extent as his stand-up career has developed. He even had a U.K. number one single for a week in 1975 with a spoof version of the Tammy Wynette song D-I-V-O-R-C-E. He also sang the theme tune to the children's television series Super Gran in 1985.

As an actor Connolly has been cast in many well-known and sometimes blockbusting films including Indecent Proposal, Muppet Treasure Island, Mrs. Brown, The Last Samurai, and Gulliver's Travels, to name a few.

Highlights:
The Frost Report
Parkinson
musical and comedic recordings
A UK number one single
Gulliver's Travels

Awards:
CBE

Tommy Cooper

Thomas Frederick Cooper was born on 19th March 1921 in Caerphilly, South Wales, and died at the age of 63 on 15th April 1984.

Tommy Cooper was rare amongst great British comedians in that he looked ridiculously funny. At 6' 4", and with a bulky physique, his appearance was large and lumbering and his look of perplexed bewilderment, especially when one of his tricks went wrong, could bring the house down.

He was also known for his red fez and his exclamation 'Just Like That', which is still one of the most famous showbiz catchphrases. That he also laughed uproariously at its own jokes only added to his puerile charm.

Cooper took up show business (after seven years of military service) on Christmas Eve in 1947 and as a member of The Magic Circle, incorporated various tricks into his act. It was only when they started to go wrong that he realised his failures were getting more laughs than his successes.

He rapidly became a variety star but it was his television work that raised him to national prominence. After his debut on the BBC talent show New to You in March 1948, he soon starred in his own shows, which became part of our television diet for four decades.

Cooper was a heavy drinker and smoker, and suffered a heart attack in 1977 while performing in Rome. By the 1980s his drinking had become a liability and the regular television work dried up.

He was also tight in other ways and was known as one of the meanest men in show business. One of his infamous stunts was to always pay the exact fare when riding in a taxi and on leaving the cab to slip something into the driver's

"Tommy Cooper was rare amongst great British comedians in that he looked ridiculously funny"

top pocket saying, 'Have a drink on me'. The taxi driver gratefully acknowledged the tip only to later find a tea bag in his pocket!

On 15th April 1984, Cooper collapsed from a heart attack in front of millions of television viewers midway through his act on the variety show Live From Her Majesty's. The audience laughed as he fell, thinking it was part of his act, until it became apparent that he was seriously ill. After much mayhem on stage, with his size-13 feet sticking out from under the curtain, he was taken to Westminster Hospital where he was pronounced dead on arrival.

In recognition of his legendary status, a statue of Cooper was unveiled in his hometown of Caerphilly, Wales, in 2008 by Oscar-winning actor Sir Anthony Hopkins, who is patron of The Tommy Cooper Society.

Highlights:
The Magic Circle
New to You
TV regular over
4 decades

"Just Like That"

Ronnie
Corbett

Ronald Balfour Corbett, CBE was born on 4th December 1930 in Edinburgh.

R onnie Corbett may only be 5' 1", but the impact he has made on the world of British comedy since the middle of the twentieth century certainly does not reflect his height! A talented comedian, actor, writer and broadcaster, Corbett is one of our much admired and adored great British comedians.

Corbett began his highly successful comedy career in the 1950s and has since been performing in all entertainment genres: film, television, radio and theatre.

Deciding to become an actor at the age of 16 after playing the part of a wicked aunt at his local church youth club, Corbett eventually began to fulfil his dream when he moved to London following his

National Service in the Royal Air Force.

Perhaps quite unusually his first roles were in films, and usually that of schoolboy roles due to his height. He was cast in the 1952 You're Only Young Once, and Top of the Form the following year.

It was whilst working at The Mayfair nightclub, however, that Corbett was spotted and was offered a part on the BBC's The Frost Report. Not only was this the major turning point in his career, but it was also the time when he first met his partner-to-be Ronnie Barker. Perhaps one of the most famous memories from the show was Class Sketch, which consisted of Corbett, Barker and John Cleese. This has in fact been one of the most repeated sketches in the history of British comedy.

Corbett's first lead role in a sitcom was then offered to him in No – That's Me Over Here! which ran from 1967 to 1970.

Corbett's own sitcom Sorry! in which he starred as Timothy Lumsden, a 40-year-old man who was still very much in the clutches of his mother, ran from 1981 to 1988. The sitcom was a great success.

The Two Ronnies ran from 1971 to 1987. Particularly memorable is when Corbett regularly sat in a huge armchair (accentuating his size, or rather lack of it), often wearing a V-necked golfing jumper and launching into hilarious comic rambling monologues.

When Barker's retirement brought an end to the Two Ronnies' era, Corbett continued on his own and has been a regular face on television and film ever since. For example, in 1997 Corbett was cast as Reggie Sea Lions, alongside John Cleese in his film Fierce Creatures. He returned to his armchair monologues in 1998 for The Ben Elton Show, and in 2005 Corbett and Barker got together again for The Two Ronnies Sketchbook, which combined comedy material from their past series with new and original material.

Corbett first received the appointment of OBE. In 2012 he was further appointed CBE for his services to entertainment and charity.

Highlights:
The Frost Report
No – That's Me
Over Here!
Sorry!
The Two Ronnies
Fierce Creatures

Awards:
OBE & CBE

Bernard
Cribbins

Bernard Cribbins, OBE was born on 29th December 1928 in Oldham, Lancashire.

Musical comedian, character actor and voice-over artist, Bernard Cribbins has been an active and celebrated performer ever since his first West End appearance in Shakespeare's A Comedy of Errors in 1956.

The seed for his career was sown in his teens, and before completing his National Service with the Parachute Regiment, Cribbins had an apprenticeship at the Oldham Repertory Theatre.

Following his West End debut Cribbins went on to co-star on the stage in Not Now Darling, There Goes the Bride, and Run for Your Wife. During this period he sang several famous comic songs including Right Said Fred and Hole in the Ground, both recorded in 1962 and released on the Parlophone record label.

Cribbins is also fondly remembered for his role as the narrator of the children's animation series The Wombles, which originally ran from 1973 to 1975. As well as being chosen to narrate a BBC's adaption of The Wind in the Willows, Cribbins became the most popular storyteller for Jackanory; between 1966 and 1991 he told 114 stories to children throughout the country.

Being cast in mostly comedy films, Cribbins has appeared on our screens since his acting career began, and performed alongside many of his contemporary and also celebrated comedy greats. His film credits include: the 1963 The Wrong Arm of the Law with Peter Sellers; he was part of the famous 'Carry On' team and appeared in three of them – Carry On Jack, Carry On Spying, and Carry On Columbus; and he was in

"The admiration and respect that Cribbins commands in the U.K. is perhaps underestimated"

the second Doctor Who film in 1966, Daleks – Invasion Earth 2150 AD. His role as the station porter Perks in the BAFTA-nominated film The Railway Children in 1970 firmly established his relationship with children's entertainment during this decade.

Cribbins' television career has been as varied and long running as his other work. His television appearances have been in successful programmes from every decade of his career: in the 1960s, The Avengers for example; Fawlty Towers in the 1970s; Worzel Gummidge and Shillingbury Tales in the 1980s; Dalziel and Pascoe in the 1990s; and in the first decade of the twenty-first century, Last of the Summer Wine and Down to Earth. Most recently he returned to the long-running children's series and played Wilfred Mott, companion of David Tennant who played the tenth Doctor in Doctor Who.

The admiration and respect that Cribbins commands in the U.K. is perhaps underestimated. When he was appointed OBE for services to drama in the 2011 Birthday Honour list, many people were up in arms that he hadn't received what he really deserved, a Knighthood.

Highlights:
West End Shows
The Wombles
The Wind in the Willows
'Carry On' films
Last of the Summer Wine

Awards:
OBE

Jimmy Cricket

Jimmy Cricket was born **James Mulgrew** on 17th October 1945 in Cookstown, County Tyrone in Northern Ireland.

Characteristically known for wearing a funny hat and having wellies on the wrong feet, Jimmy Cricket is still very much one of our active British comedians, and has been making people laugh since the 1960s.

Having left school at the age of 16, Cricket spent the first two years of his working life in a betting shop. He spent the summer of 1966 working as a Redcoat in the County Meath Butlins holiday camp. He then moved to Clacton-on-Sea in Essex where he worked for a further two seasons as a Redcoat. It was during this time that he began accumulating a comedy 'patter' which, with his Irish way, seemed to make the Brits chortle.

Cricket, having moved to Manchester, defected and became a Bluecoat at the Pontins holiday camps in Southport and Morecambe from 1972. This is in fact where he met his wife and in his characteristic humorous style described the first time he met her: 'When I bumped into her she was wearing a Halloween mask, it was love at first fright'!

Having spent time developing his comedy style and character on the northern comedy club circuit, the real turning point in his career came after he won Search For A Star, the London Weekend Television talent contest. This exposure led to his own television series in the mid-1980s called And There's More, which was broadcast on Central Television.

Quickly becoming a household name and family favourite, Cricket was appearing regularly as a guest on televi-

"still very much one of our active British comedians, and has been making people laugh since the 1960s"

sion and radio shows. He then had his own BBC Radio 2 programme, and performed alongside the likes of The Krankies in The Krankies Klub and contemporary comedian Bobby Davro.

Cricket's Irish humour has always been totally clean, unlike many of his comic contemporaries! His live performances therefore reach out to everyone, from children to great-grandmothers; he can quite literally make anyone giggle, and without causing the slightest bit of offence.

His most famous catchphrases are 'come closer!' and '… and there's more!' A lot of his material comes from the theme of Irish logic, and of course there are the renowned 'Letters from Mammy'. Most recently Cricket has written his first musical Let's Hear it for the Wee Man. It is a moving story about Jim Magennis, an Irish submariner who was the last Northern Irishman to be decorated with the Victoria Cross. The musical was premiered on St. Patrick's Day at the Thwaites Empire Theatre in Blackburn in 2011.

Cricket continues to tour the country with his comic live performances, is in demand for private engagements and also performs regularly for charity events.

Highlights:
Winning Search For A Star
And There's More
His own BBC Radio 2 programme
Let's Hear it for the Wee Man

"Come closer"
"… and there's more!"

Les Dawson

Leslie Dawson was born on 2nd February 1931 in Manchester, and died at the age of 62 on 10th June 1993.

" **My name is Les Dawson. That's a stage name actually, I was christened Friday Dawson because when my father saw me he said to my mother 'I think we'd better call it a day'.** "

Dawson claimed that he began his entertainment career as a pianist in a Parisian brothel: 'I finally heard some applause from a bald man and said "thank you for clapping me" and he said "I'm not clapping – I'm slapping me head to keep awake"'.

He turned to comedy, however, when he found he got laughs by playing wrong notes and moaning about his lot to the audience.

He was an instant hit on his television debut on the talent show Opportunity Knocks in 1967 and he remained as one of the country's best-loved comics for the rest of his life.

His most popular routine featured Roy Barraclough with the two of them dressed as two elderly Lancastrian women, Cissie Braithwaite and Ada Shufflebotham. Cissie had pretensions of refinement and often corrected Ada's malapropisms or vulgar expressions. As authentic characters of their day, they spoke some words aloud but only mouthed others, particularly those pertaining to bodily functions and sex. At one time, no respectable woman would have said, for instance, 'She's having a hysterectomy'. Instead they would have mouthed, 'She's having women's troubles'. (Dawson's character, of course, mistakenly said 'hysterical rectumy.')

These female characters were based on those Les Dawson knew in real life. He explained that this mouthing of words (or 'mee-mawing') was a habit of Lancashire millworkers trying to communicate over the tremendous racket of the looms, which was also resorted to in daily life for indelicate subjects. To further portray the reality of northern, working-class women, Cissie and Ada would sit with folded arms, occasionally adjusting their bosoms by a hoist of the forearms.

Dawson loved to undercut his own fondness for high culture. For example, he was a talented pianist but developed a gag where he would begin to play a familiar piece such as Beethoven's Moonlight Sonata. After he had established the identity of the piece being performed, Dawson would introduce

pockmarked Lascar in the arms of a frump in a Huddersfield bordello …'

He was also a master of painting a beautiful word picture and then letting the audience down with a bump: 'The other day I was gazing up at the night sky, a purple vault fretted with a myriad points of light twinkling in wondrous formation, while shooting stars streaked across the heavens, and I thought, I really must repair the roof on this toilet.'

One of his last television appearances came on 23rd December 1992, when he appeared as special guest on the TV

Highlights:
Opportunity
Knocks
Cissie Braithwaite
and Ada
Shufflebotham
Apperared twice
on This Is Your
Life

"I'm not clapping – I'm slapping me head to keep awake"

hideously wrong notes (yet not to the extent of destroying the identity of the tune) without appearing to realise that he had done so, meanwhile smiling unctuously and apparently relishing the accuracy and soul of his own performance.

His love of language (Dawson wrote many novels) influenced many of his comedy routines. For example, he started one fairly routine joke with the line 'I was vouchsafed this vision by a

guest show This Is Your Life – 21 years after previously appearing as the show's special guest – making him one of the few people to appear on the show twice.

On 10th June 1993, during a checkup at a hospital in Whalley Range, Manchester, Les Dawson died suddenly after suffering a heart attack. Many comedians and other celebrities attended a memorial service for him at Westminster Abbey on 24th February 1994.

Ken Dodd

Kenneth Arthur Dodd, OBE was born in Knotty Ash, Liverpool on 8th November 1927.

Famous for his frizzy hair and buck teeth, Ken Dodd is one of the last of the dying breed of variety performers who has been tickling funny bones for nearly 60 years.

His style is shotgun fast and relies on the rapid delivery of one-liner jokes although he intersperses his act with occasional songs, both serious and humorous, in an incongruously fine light baritone voice.

Dodd is renowned for the length of his performances, and during the 1960s he earned a place in the Guinness Book of Records for the world's longest ever joke-telling session: 1,500 jokes in three and a half hours undertaken at a Liverpool theatre, where audiences were observed going in and out in shifts.

He was born in November 1927 in Knotty Ash, Liverpool, and started entertaining in his teens as a ventriloquist at local venues. He got his big break in 1954, aged 26, when he made his professional show-business debut at the now-demolished Nottingham Empire.

While his quick fire repartee was made for radio and television, he was really in his element with the buzz of a live audience. Indeed, he enjoyed the longest ever 42-week run at the London Palladium in 1965, which broke all box office records.

In a bid to reach the younger members of his audiences, Dodd created the Diddymen, a fictionalised family from Knotty Ash that included Dicky Mint, Mick the Marmaliser, Hamish McDiddy, and Neil Ponsonby-Smallpiece. Although puppets were used for his television shows, children or midgets portrayed the Diddymen during their annual Christmas concerts.

Ken also enjoyed a number of chart hits in the mid-60s most notably with Tears, which sold over two million copies, Promises, and sugar sweet songs such as Happiness, which became his theme tune.

He was awarded the OBE in the 1982 Queen's Honours List for his services to entertainment and charity, but by the end of the decade he was employing Queen's Counsel after he was charged with tax evasion.

Defended by George Carman DC, he was acquitted but couldn't resist using the experience in his stage acts introducing himself by saying: 'Good evening, my name is Kenneth Arthur Dodd: singer, photographic playboy and failed accountant'.

In a 2005 poll of comedians to find 'The Comedian's Comedian' he was voted amongst the 'Top 50 Comedy Acts Ever'. A statue depicting Dodd with his trademark feather duster was unveiled in Lime Street Station, Liverpool in June 2009.

Highlights:
longest ever
42-week run
at the London
Palladium in 1965
The Diddymen
Many chart hits
Guinness Book of
Records for the
world's longest
ever joke-telling
session

Awards:
OBE

Dick Emery

Richard Gilbert Emery was born on 19th February 1915 in Bloomsbury, London. He died at the age of 67 on 2nd January 1983.

Widely known for his phrase 'Ooh, you are awful – but I like you', Dick Emery became a legendary British comedian who has not only had a profound influence on some of today's comedians and comedy shows, but he created and developed unique comedy characters for which he will always be affectionately remembered.

Acting and comedy was no doubt in Emery's blood as he was the son of the comedy double act Callan and Emery. He did not, however, know immediately that this was his calling, and he had several jobs before embarking on his comic career.

Emery was called up to the RAF during World War II. Preferring to be on the stage, however, Emery deserted and joined the cast of The Merry Widow at the Majestic Theatre in London; he was subsequently arrested and incarcerated.

With the war over Emery joined the Windmill Theatre. It wasn't long before he became a regular on radio and television, and he appeared on various programmes throughout the 1950s including Educating Archie. Tony Hancock was a close friend of Emery, and he joined him in The Tony Hancock Show from 1956 to 1957, and Hancock's Half Hour, which ran from 1956 to 1960.

The real turning point in Emery's career and the period in his life that established him as a much loved household name were due to the BBC offering him an exclusive contract for The Dick Emery Show. The show ran from 1963 to 1981 and gave Emery the freedom to develop a plethora of new characters,

"He created and developed *unique* comedy *characters* for which he will always be *affectionately remembered*"

with which he will always be associated.

In 1972, due to the success of his comedy show, the BBC named him their television personality of the year.

His film work was less consistent than his radio and television work. He did, however, appear in 10 films between 1956 and 1972. His debut was in the Goons' The Case of the Mukkinese Battlehorn, and, widely regarded as his best film performance, was his role as Booky Binns, the clumsy bank robber in the 1965 film The Big Job. Emery's voice also enhanced his popularity; in particular his contribution to the Beatles' Yellow Submarine gave him cult status.

Having moved to ITV at the end of the 1970s for three one-hour specials, Emery returned to the BBC for, what were to be, the last years of his life. First reigniting The Dick Emery Show, then with the new character Jewish private detective Bernie Weinstock created, two series of Emery Presents were broadcast just before his death in 1983.

Emery's success and comic style has had a significant influence on many more recent comic actors including Harry Enfield, Paul Whitehouse, and Matt Lucas and David Walliams in the comedy series Little Britain.

Highlights:
The Merry Widow
Educating Archie
Hancock's
Half Hour
The Dick Emery
Show
The Case of
the Mukkinese
Battlehorn
The Big Job

"Ooh, you are awful - but I like you"

George Formby

George Formby, OBE was born **George Hoy Booth** on 26th May 1904 in Wigan, Lancashire. He died at the age of 56 on 6th March 1961.

One of our earliest British comedy great stars, George Formby made his name as a comedian, singer-song-writer, actor and entertainer on stage and on screen during the 1930s and 1940s, and his show business career spanned precisely 40 years. Formby's comic and sometime risqué vocals for the time, accompanied by him on the banjo ukulele (or banjulele as it was also known) became his trademark.

Born to a very successful music hall comedian in his own right, James Booth, Formby only first moved to the stage after the death of his father. He began his career using his father's comic repertoire, which was not a successful start. It wasn't until Formby got hold of the banjo ukulele that he developed a unique musical style,

and combined it with his Lancashire accent and cheeky humour. Now he began to stand out from the crowd.

Formby contributed to and performed over 300 songs during his lifetime. His first record successes came in 1932 when he performed with the famous Jack Hylton Band. It was the B-side song, Chinese Blues, later renamed Chinese Laundry Blues that was a hit, and became Formby's signature tune.

From his stage performances, his most well-known phrases include 'Turned out nice again!' and 'Eeh, isn't it grand!' Not only was he the most popular British entertainer of his era, he was also the highest paid, and by 1939 he was earning more than £100,000 a year.

Musically, Formby created a style of his own. It became so synonymous with him due to its highly syncopated style, combined with his innocent, high-pitched and nasal accent, that it was labelled the 'Formby style'. With this he combined his own take on northern English country humour, which all together was unique, new and highly popular.

Formby also became quite a film star during his lifetime and this side of his career was launched following the first film he made in 1934, Boots! Boots! This led to Elstree Studios offering him an 11-film contract. Columbia Studios later offered him a further seven-film contract, worth some £500,000. Out of each film invariably came three or four songs that would then be released on sheet music and as 78-rpm records. Songs such as Fanlight Fanny, The Window Cleaner, and one of his most famous songs Leaning on a Lamp Post, written by Noel Gay, were the results of Formby's film work. His comedy film Let George Do It, was and probably still is, the most successful and popular of his entire screen output.

During World War II Formby joined the Entertainments National Service Association (ENSA) and travelled Europe and North Africa entertaining the troops.

Following a heart attack in 1951 whilst in the middle of the musical show Zip Goes a Million in the West End, Formby started slowing down his entertainment schedule whilst recuperating. His last record, Happy Go Lucky Me, and his last television programme, The Friday Show, were made in 1960. Formby suffered another heart attack the following year, which he did not recover from.

Highlights:
Successful music hall comedian
Contributed to over 300 songs including;
The Window Cleaner
Columbia Studios Fims

Awards:
OBE

Bill Fraser

William Simpson Fraser was born on 5th June 1908 in Perth, Scotland. He died at the age of 79 on 9th September 1987.

Scottish comic and character actor Bill Fraser was a part of British theatre, film and television for nearly 50 years, and he had a career that spanned everything from pantomime to Shakespeare.

It was tough at the start when he couldn't find acting work and he even slept on the Embankment in London when things were really bad financially. He then secured the job of running the Connaught Theatre in Worthing. He then met Eric Sykes during World War II whilst serving in the Royal Air Force; in fact he got Sykes his first radio writing job. The two remained lifelong friends and worked together frequently throughout their entertainment careers.

It was his popularity and success on television that earned him an enduring place in the hearts of British audiences. His first appearance was in 1956 on The Tony Hancock Show, after which he became a regular part of the Hancock's Half Hour team. Particularly pivotal in terms of his career was his role as Sergeant Claude Snudge in The Army Game. The black-and-white comedy sitcom was broadcast on ITV from 1957 to 1961 and was based on the theme of National Service conscription to the British Army. Its sequel, Bootsie and Snudge, originally ran from 1960 to 1964.

Firmly established as one of the great British comic actors of his era, Fraser went on to appear in many comedy television productions including The Secret Diary of Adrian Mole, Aged 13¾, Foreign Affairs, and Father, Dear Father.

Although he had 48 years in and

*"Part of **British theatre**, **film** and **television** for nearly 50 years, and he had a career that spanned everything from **pantomime** to **Shakespeare**"*

around the movie business, his film output was not as prolific as perhaps it could have been, with on average about one film per year. Having said that, there are several successful comedy films in which Fraser was involved. For example, Doctors at Large in 1957, The Amorous Milkman in 1975, and the Frankie Howerd trilogy, Up Pompeii!, Up the Front, and Up the Chastity Belt.

Fraser was also a respected serious actor and he was cast in numerous television and some film roles as such, from playing Judge Roger Bullingham in the British television series Rumpole of the Bailey, Mr Micawber in the 1966 dramatisation of David Copperfield, to his final performance as Mr Casby in the film adaptation of Dickens' novel, Little Dorrit, which was broadcast a year after Fraser's death in 1988.

Highlights:
Hancock's Half
Hour team
The Army Game
Bootsie and
Snudge
The Secret Diary
of Adrian Mole
Doctors at Large

French and *Saunders*

Dawn Roma French was born on 11th October 1957 in Holyhead, Wales.

Jennifer Jane Saunders was born on 6th July 1958 in Sleaford, Lincolnshire.

The comic duo Dawn French and Jennifer Saunders are arguably the most successful pair of British female comedians of the modern era. Famously known for their comedy sketch television show of the same name, French and Saunders, they are responsible for both writing and starring in it.

French and Saunders first met at the Central School of Speech and Drama in 1978 and they began collaborating from the word go. They were spotted whilst performing at the London comedy club The Comic Strip in the 1980s. As part of an increasing underground comedy scene, alongside the likes of Miranda Richardson and Alan Rickman, they were soon an established pair and ready for the launch to stardom that followed.

French and Saunders were at the height of British comedy popularity during the late 1980s and early 1990s. Due to the success and fast growing ratings of the series, the BBC in fact gave the show one of the highest budgets in their history, enabling the comic pair to create detailed spoofs, satires and parodies of popular mainstream culture. Originally the series was run from 1987 to 2007 with 46 episodes.

Apart from their television series, they have produced numerous Christmas and Comic Relief Specials over the years. Although not done regularly, they have also taken their comedy sketch show on a tour of the U.K. only three times in its history – in 1990, 2000, and 2008.

In addition to French and Saunders they have worked together on several other productions and series over

"Dawn **French** *and* Jennifer **Saunders** *are arguably the* **most successful** *pair of* **British female comedians** *of the modern era"*

the years including The Comic Strip Presents from 1982 to 1998, Girls On Top from 1985 to 1986, and Jam & Jerusalem from 2006 to 2009.

Individually they have also both had remarkable success as comediennes in their own right and have both won BAFTA Fellowships.

Most notably Dawn French has starred on television in: Murder Most Horrid; the extremely popular sitcom The Vicar of Dibley; Wild West; Lark Rise to Candleford; and Psychoville. Her film roles include David Copperfield, Harry Potter and the Prisoner of Azkaban, and The Chronicles of Narnia: The Lion, the Witch and the Wardrobe to name a few. French has been nominated for seven

BAFTA Awards so far in her career.

Jennifer Saunders is most famously known for writing, and for her role as Edina Monsoon, in Absolutely Fabulous, which began in 1992. She has also appeared in box office hit films including Muppet Treasure Island and Spice World (the Spice Girls' film). She is also much admired for her voiceover work in Shrek 2, where Saunders was the voice of Princess Fiona's evil Fairy Godmother.

Saunders has won two BAFTAs, a British Comedy Award, an International Emmy Award, a People's Choice Award, and two Writers' Guild of Great Britain Awards.

Stephen Fry

Stephen John Fry was born on 24th August 1957 in Hampstead, London.

Actor, comedian, novelist, columnist, screenwriter, poet, presenter, noted wit, vocal gay rights advocate, and general bon vivant. Stephen Fry is one of the most versatile and outspoken talents to come along in the latter half of the twentieth century.

Since beginning his creative partnership with Hugh Laurie in 1981, Fry has become an established British television personality, a regular and recognisable voice on radio, a witty and sometimes controversial voice in the media, and a critically acclaimed author.

Life didn't start quite as smoothly for Fry, however, and it wasn't until he won a scholarship to Queen's College Cambridge to read English Literature, that he saw the light and began towing the society line.

Becoming involved with the famous Cambridge Footlights Revue cast (alongside the likes of Hugh Laurie, Emma Thompson and Tony Slattery), Fry came to prominence with the others in 1981 following the Footlights' performance of The Cellar Tapes. Written by Fry and Laurie, the revue not only won the first ever Edinburgh Festival Fringe Perrier Award, but it was broadcast on BBC 2 the following year.

Some of Fry's most notable television work includes A Bit of Fry and Laurie for which Fry co-wrote and co-starred alongside Laurie in the comedy sketch series that originally ran from 1989 to 1995. He played the part of Melchett in Rowan Atkinson's Blackadder series, and was Jeeves in Jeeves and Wooster, which ran from 1990 to 1993.

Fry's contribution to the big screen has also been fairly prolific. He has appeared in films such as A Fish Called Wanda (1988) and the same year's A Handful of Dust. Perhaps his most memorable film performances are, however, in Peter's Friends, in which Fry co-starred with Emma Thompson, Kenneth Branagh, and various members of the Footlights set; John Schlesinger's Cold Comfort Farm; Wilde, a bibliographical British film about Oscar Wilde; the musical comedy film starring the Spice Girls, Spice World; and A Civil Action. His most recent film role will be in the new making of the J. R. Tolkien's classic book, The Hobbit, in which he is cast as Master of Lake-town.

Fry received particular attention for his work in Wilde, owing both to the filmmakers' decision not to gloss over the details of the Victorian playwright's sex life, and to Fry's uncanny physical resemblance to Oscar Wilde.

As well as being the charismatic voice of the Harry Potter audiobooks, Fry is a familiar sound on the radio and is a regular on programmes such as Radio 4's I'm Sorry I Haven't a Clue and Just a Minute. As a writer Fry has two autobiographies and four novels published. He also writes regular columns for newspapers and magazines.

Highlights:
Footlights Revue
The Cellar Tapes
A Bit of Fry and Laurie
Blackadder
Jeeves and Wooster

The Goodies

Timothy Julian Brooke-Taylor, OBE was born on 17th July 1940 in Buxton, Derbyshire.

David Graeme Garden, OBE was born on 18th February 1943 in Aberdeen.

William Edgar Oddie, OBE was born on 7th July 1941 in Rochdale, Greater Manchester.

The hugely popular British comedy trio, The Goodies, created often surreal comedy sketches and were at the height of popularity during the 1970s and early 1980s. The talented protagonists of the trio were Tim Brooke-Taylor, Graeme Garden and Bill Oddie, all of whom have had and continue to have successful solo show business careers in their own right.

All three were at Cambridge University and met when they all joined the Cambridge University Footlights Club. This period in Footlights' history was evidently the nursery for many a great comedy creation to come. Also in the group at the same time were John Cleese, Graham Chapman and Eric Idle.

All three of The Goodies-to-be started their professional comedy careers by performing on the successful 1960s BBC radio comedy show I'm Sorry, I'll Read That Again. The programme was in fact the result of the 1963 Footlights revue entitled A Clump of Plinths, later renamed Cambridge Circus.

Individually, they also appeared in various shows during this pre-Goodie era. Brooke-Taylor was in the satirical television show At Last the 1948 Show and the comedy sketch series Marty. Garden and Oddie were cast in the comedy sketch radio series Twice a Fortnight. All three then came together in 1968 and starred in (what became the precursor to The Goodies) the BBC television comedy series Broaden Your Mind.

In 1970 the first episode of The Goodies was broadcast on BBC 2. All three Goodies contributed to writing the series (as well as starring in it), which was a combination of situation comedy and surreal sketches. Oddie also wrote most of the songs and music for the series, and co-wrote the theme tune with Michael Gibbs. The Goodies was hugely successful and ran for a total of 76 episodes until 1980 with the BBC, then moved to ITV from 1980 to 1981.

LEFT The Goodies in the 1970s

With the tagline 'We Do Anything, Anywhere, Anytime', the basic format of the series featured the hard-up trio offering themselves for hire. This inevitably created an open platform for all kinds of off-the-wall comedy scenarios to arise. They often parodied current affairs, pop music, etc., whilst other story lines would be more surreal and abstractly philosophical. The use of slapstick humour, clever (albeit low-budget) visual effects and sped-up photography all contributed to this unique series.

Some critics thought that The Goodies was too juvenile, particularly in comparison with other contemporary comedy series, such as Monty Python's Flying Circus. The British audience, however, begged to differ as the series appealed to both adults (on an intellectual level) and also children, due to its slapstick and visual humour. It was not only popular in the U.K., and the series (sometimes in part) travelled successfully to Australia, Canada, Germany, Spain, the U.S. and New Zealand.

The trio cite economic reasons for the eventual cancellation of their series; each episode cost quite a bit more to create than other contemporary shows.

Whilst Brooke-Taylor and Garden received OBEs in 2011 for services to light entertainment, Oddie received his for wildlife conservation in 2003.

Highlights:
BBC radio comedy show I'm Sorry, I'll Read That Again
Broaden Your Mind

Tony Hancock

Anthony John Hancock was born on 12th May 1924 in Hall Green, Birmingham. He died at the age of 44 on 24th June 1968.

One of the most successful British comedians at the height of his popularity in the 1950s and early 1960s, Tony Hancock pushed the boundaries of British comedy at the time. Unfortunately he lost his way due to work, marital and alcohol problems and committed suicide at the age of 44. It was a very sad end for one of our country's most brilliant comedians.

Hancock's first dealings with a stage occurred during World War II when, having joined the Royal Air Force, he became part of the Ralph Reader Gang Show. Working at the Windmill Theatre in London as a resident comedian sometime after the war helped launch his career, as it did for many of his contemporaries at the time. From here Hancock got his first radio work and appeared on Workers' Playtime and Variety Bandbox for example.

His successful radio work naturally led to television work, and in the early 1950s he was cast in Educating Archie and made regular appearances in the light entertainment show Kaleidoscope. Hancock was quickly becoming both recognised and popular.

Hancock cemented his relationship with British radio and television audiences as a hugely popular comedian when the BBC offered him his own radio programme, Hancock's Half Hour. It was first broadcast in 1954 and a total of six series of over 100 episodes were aired. Other well-known personalities were involved in the radio series including Sid James, Hattie Jacques, Bill Kerr and Kenneth Williams.

The series was hugely successful and it is credited as being a major contributor to the development of the genre of the sitcom as we know it today. Prior to Hancock's Half Hour, comedy radio shows had focused on a combination of sketches, musical interludes and guest appearances. This was the first time that an entire storyline was presented, developed and concluded in one half-hour episode.

The BBC television version of Hancock's Half Hour began in 1956 and a total of seven series were broadcast. At the time, comedy programmes like this were broadcast live, but due to Hancock's unpredictable temperament, his shows were pre-recorded. The television episodes alternated with the radio programmes until 1959, and then the fifth television series and the final radio series were broadcast simultaneously that autumn.

Written by Ray Galton and Alan Simpson, Sid James was Hancock's co-star in the radio and television version until 1960. Hancock decided that he no longer needed James and did not like the fact that the public viewed him as part of a double act. He created one final television series called simply Hancock, which he performed alone. In fact some of Hancock's most popular and enduring episodes came out of this final series including The Blood Donor and The Radio Ham.

Having rejected Sid James, Hancock then rejected his writers in 1961. Although he continued to appear fairly regularly on British television until 1967, depression and alcoholism were taking their toll. He went to Sydney the following year to record a 13-part Hancock Down Under series, but this was not to be. He committed suicide whilst there having only recorded three programmes.

Highlights:
Kaleidoscope
Hancock's
Half Hour
The Blood Donor
The Radio Ham
**Hancock Down
Under series**

Will Hay

William Thomson Hay was born on 6th December 1888 in Stockton-On-Tees. He died at the age of 60 on 18th April 1949.

Originally a music-hall performer, who turned into a much loved and popular comedy star, Will Hay was also a respected actor and film director, as well as being a serious amateur astronomer in his spare time. Voted by British film exhibitors in the annual poll of British film stars in the Motion Picture Herald, Hay was in the top 10 three years in a row from 1936 to 1938.

Having started life as an engineer, Hay turned to the stage when he was 21 and established himself as a well-known and talented music-hall artist. On stage he became synonymous with the role of an inept schoolmaster. This later led to several film roles where he was portrayed in a similar vein.

Following from his stage performances, the roles for films that characterised him as a schoolmaster who couldn't keep his pupils in order included the 1935 Boys Will Be Boys, and Good Morning, Boys! in 1937.

By the late 1930s Hay had become a comedy star on the big screen and worked closely with Graham Moffat and veteran actor Moore Marriott on a number of films. The first collaboration for which Hay co-wrote the script was the 1937 film, Windbag the Sailor. The comic and charismatic interplay between the three different actors was the start of a series of comedies that were extremely popular. Produced by Gainsborough Pictures, the full team consisted of director Marcel Varnel and writers Val Guest and Marriott Edgar, with Marriott and Moffat as Hay's supporting actors. The ensuing

"Originally a music-hall performer, who turned into a **much loved** *and popular* **comedy star**, *Will Hay was also a* **respected actor** *and* **film director"**

films, including Oh, Mr. Porter! in 1937, Convict in 1938, Old Bones of the River in 1939, and Ask a Policeman also in 1939, were not only comically wonderful, but were made with great care from the photography through to the sets.

In 1941 Hay moved to Ealing Studios and broke up the Marriott and Moffat trio. Now starring on his own and co-directing with Basil Dearden, the following three films were released: The Goose Steps Out and The Black Sheep of Whitehall in 1942, and My Learned Friend in 1943. Some would argue that Hay's performances were never quite the same after the Marriott and Moffat split, although his final film My Learned Friend, is widely regarded as one of his crowning career performances, as well as the film being considered a masterpiece of black comedy.

Highlights:
Boys Will Be Boys
Windbag the Sailor
Oh, Mr. Porter!
Old Bones of the River
Ask a Policeman

Benny Hill

Alfred Hawthorne Hill was born on 21st January 1924 in Southampton, Hampshire. He died at the age of 68 on 20th April 1992.

One of Britain's most celebrated and successful comedians ever, Benny Hill was an innovative leader in the development of comedy and was seen as a star for more than 40 years. He was also the first British comedian to make his name and fortune through television alone.

Hill became acquainted with the stage during World War II when he performed in variety shows to entertain the troops. He also dipped his toe into radio occasionally, on Beginners Please and Petticoat Lane (You Want It, We've Got It) for example.

It was through his experience on television shows such as Mud in Your Eyes in 1950, Hi There! in 1951, and particularly variety shows such as Starlight Symphony in 1951 and The Services Show in 1953 that facilitated his development of the parody sketch show. This cemented his comedy style and with it his popularity.

Written by Hill and Dave Freeman, The Benny Hill Show ran from 1955 to 1968. The highly successful format of the show revolved around parody, often involving well-known personalities, existing television shows and social trends at the time. Hill's love of silent comedy also influenced his show and, combined with his innuendo-laden comic songs, mimed sketches played an important part.

Hill is now famously and fondly remembered for his naughtiness. The saucy, sex-obsessed side of Hill's comedy, that involved him being surrounded or chasing scantily clad young ladies, was a development that came

"Hill is now famously and fondly remembered for his naughtiness"

later however.

Hill had, for the first part of his career, been working predominantly with the BBC. He then moved to ITV in 1969 and stayed with Thames Television for the latter half of his career. It is during this period that Hill's emphasis on sexual innuendo and the suspender-adorned ladies began to play a major role in his comedy scripts, which incidentally he was now writing alone. It is perhaps a shame that this is the enduring memory of Hill's comedy for which he is posthumously remembered. In fact as he got older, having once been fondly regarded as just a naughty boy, this image gradually changed to a dirty old man!

Hill's emphasis and use of visual humour also meant that his comedy was appreciated internationally as it didn't rely on audiences necessarily being able to speak English. Not only was he one of Britain's most popular comedians ever, but also his television shows were broadcast in over 100 countries throughout the world.

Viewers voted Hill television personality of the year for 1954 such was his popularity. He won the BBC's Personality of the Year Award in 1965. He even had a Christmas number one hit in 1971 with the single Ernie (The Fastest Milkman in the West). For Hill personally, however, the award he was most proud of and received a year before his death was the aptly titled Charlie Chaplin International Award for Comedy.

Highlights:
Mud in Your Eyes
Starlight
Symphony
The Benny
Hill Show
Christmas number
one hit in 1971

Awards:
Television
personality of
the year 1954
BBC's Personality
of the Year
Award in 1965

Hinge and *Bracket*

George Logan
was born on
7th July 1944
in Rutherglen,
Scotland.

Patrick Fyffe
was born on
23rd January
1942 in Stafford,
Staffordshire. He
died at the age of
60 on 11th May
2002.

British impersonation artists George Logan and Patrick Fyffe played the two old comic and eccentric spinsters Dr. Evadne Hinge and Dame Hilda Bracket respectively. Between 1972 and 2001 they were a popular part of the British comedy scene on radio and television, and on the stage.

The basis for the duo's creation of the characters was that the two old spinsters, living quiet lives in the village of Stackton Tressel, continued to celebrate their earlier careers on the provincial operatic stage. This is how it all began, with their early appearances playing out their initial return to the stage to perform concerts 'by popular request'.

Both talented musicians as well as comedy actors, their act included singing recitals with Logan as accompanist and arranger for Fyffe's vocal performances, which were sung exclusively in falsetto. The interaction between the two consisted of musical numbers interspersed with hilarious comic anecdotes and spinsterish bickering; this was the basic structure that created a powerful dynamic.

Unlike most other comedy duo acts, the Hinge and Bracket performances created a real sense of theatrical history that developed for almost 30 years. These were not just two performers who got together for the occasional comedy show. Their entire career together (as Hinge and Bracket) portrayed a convincing and comic picture for the audience, including historic details of the ladies' genteel lifestyle.

Small but massively effective use of language gave authenticity to this, such

"Hinge and Bracket performances created a real sense of theatrical history"

as the fact that they always referred to each other as 'Dear'. A further example of how the pair created the believable historical context for their act (and pecking order) happened early on when Dame Hilda explains their titles to the audience: her own damehood was awarded for 'services to music and opera', whereas Evadne's Dr. was bestowed 'for hard work'.

Naturally, Logan and Fyffe were always immaculately and authentically turned out in drag, and they even went as far as to refuse any interaction with the media when they were out of character. This ingeniously breathed an aspect of real life and longevity into

the characters and made it possible for audiences to really get to know them, as if they really were real people.

Following the death of Fyffe in 2002, Logan retired from the stage two years later having decided that Dr. Evadne Hinge could simply no longer exist as an isolated character. In tribute to his lifelong stage partner Logan said that Fyffe was 'fabulously talented, a brilliant clown and a natural comedian. Since Patrick is no longer with us, [Hinge and Bracket] can never happen again. When you've worked with the best, there'd be no point in doing second best afterwards, so I'd rather leave it as it is.'

Highlights:
Talented
musicians as
well as
comedy actors
Radio and
television and
stage success

Frankie Howerd

Francis Alick Howerd, OBE was born on 6th March 1917 in York. He died at the age of 75 on 19th April 1992.

Sometimes regarded as the comedian and comic actor who always bounced back, Frankie Howerd is one of Britain's most admired and remembered comedians who touched audiences of different generations for over 50 years.

As with many of his contemporaries born in this era, Howerd's first taste of performing began during World War II with entertainment shows for the troops. He then came into the public arena initially on the radio between 1946 and 1950 on the show Variety Bandbox.

During this radio work, Howerd worked closely with Eric Sykes, and this relationship proved very successful, with Sykes continuing to write most of his material throughout the 1950s. Moving to television in 1952, the three-part series The Howerd Crowd was the first. This was followed by programmes such as Nuts in May and The Frankie Howerd Show, the latter of which also had the input of Spike Milligan.

Film and theatre also became part of Howerd's performing arsenal in the 1950s and he appeared in stage productions such as Charley's Aunt and The Perfect Woman. Cinematically he was cast in The Runaway Bus, The Ladykillers, and Jumping for Joy for example. Howerd's career seemed to be going very well indeed. By the end of the decade, however, he was being regarded as a bit 'last year', 'old hat' and difficult to work with.

It was not until 1962 that his first resurgence occurred. Having successfully pleased the audiences at Peter Cook's The Establishment Club in London, he was booked the following year by Ned Sherrin for the BBC satire show, That Was The Week That Was. This was the catalyst that put his television career back on track.

Between 1964 and 1966 Howerd's

that the popularity of Howerd in these underling roles, that had been initially so well received, was on the gradual decline.

Howerd's comedy trademark was when he talked directly to the audience interspersed with his most famous phrases 'Ooooh, no missus' and 'Titter ye not'! He was also renowned for pretending that he didn't know what the audience were laughing at, when he had obviously just blurted out glaring double entendres.

By the late 1970s and early 1980s, Howerd's humour was once again being viewed as out of date. He was awarded an OBE in 1977, however. Coming back again from a lull, he found a new audience this time – younger people, particularly students. This was augmented all the more when ITV broadcast Frankie Howerd on Campus in 1990, as he performed to an audience of giggling students at the Oxford Union.

Howerd died from heart failure the day before his good friend and fellow comedian Benny Hill did.

popularity continued with similar satirical shows such as A Last Word on the Election and the series Frankie Howerd. In fact as it turned out, situation comedy was to prove his most successful. Several television sitcom productions followed such as Up Pompeii, Further Up Pompeii, Whoops Baghdad, and A Touch of the Casanovas. It has to be said, however,

Highlights:
Variety Bandbox
The Frankie Howerd Show
The Runaway Bus
The series Frankie Howerd

Awards:
OBE

Eddie Izzard

Edward John Izzard was born on 7th February 1962 in Aden, Yemen (at the time of his birth the Colony of Aden in the Aden Protectorate).

Ingenious, unique and absolutely hilarious, Eddie Izzard is one of British comedy's modern legends in the making. Apart from being one of the most famous transvestites in the country, his sometimes surreal, bizarre, observational and improvised narratives cover all manner of subject material from popular culture to sex and religion to the latest box office films.

Izzard 'played' with comedy whilst at the University of Sheffield, but the seed had been sown. In fact, he didn't finish his accountancy degree and instead turned to doing comedy street performances in Europe and the U.S. His first gig in a proper comedy venue was at the Banana Cabaret club in Balham, London. This was followed by his first real 'on stage' performance in 1987 at The Comedy Store. The final years of the 1980s and early 1990s saw Izzard refine his comedy material and improvisational style that he had been developing throughout the previous decade, and he was well on the road to recognition.

His break into the mainstream British comedy world both on stage and on television came following his delivery of his 'Wolves' sketch on Fry and Laurie in 1991 as part of their AIDS benefit show, Hysteria 3. From there on in he gained an enormous following and fan club that not only stretches across the world, but also crosses social and cultural boundaries.

Many of Izzard's live performances are famous. A sample of his most notable includes Live at the Ambassadors (his West End debut), Definite Article, Dress to Kill, Glorious, and Circle.

Izzard has that effect on his audiences that means, once addicted and infected by Izzard humour, the rest of one's life is spent unconsciously throwing 'Izzardisms' flippantly into conversation with friends and family, sometimes to the bemusement of whoever is listening if they are not a fan!

Predominantly influenced by comedians such as Spike Milligan and the Monty Python team, Cleese himself has even referred to Izzard as the 'Lost Python'. Izzard's stand-up comedy style is based on improvising, yet moving from subject to subject in streams of consciousness. His is also a talented mimic and mime artist and can do brilliant impressions of famous people, characters and inanimate objects.

Izzard's television and film appearances are also not to be sneezed at. He played the starring role as Wayne Malloy in the FX television series The Riches. Film-wise, and to name a few, he has been in Ocean's Twelve, Ocean's Thirteen, Mystery Men, Shadow of the Vampire, Across the Universe, The Chronicles of Narnia: Prince Caspian, and Valkyrie.

To date Izzard has received two Emmy Awards for the 2000 Dress to Kill performance, as well as two British Comedy Awards, the first in 1993 for Top Stand-up following Live at the Ambassadors, and in 1996 with Best Stand-up for Definite Article.

Highlights:
Live at the Ambassadors
The Riches
The Chronicles of Narnia
Prince Caspian
Dress to Kill

Awards:
Two Emmy Awards
Two British Comedy Awards

"Ingenious, unique and absolutely hilarious"

Sid James

Sid James was born **Solomon Joel Cohen** on 8th May 1913 in Hillbrow, Johannesburg. He died at the age of 62 on 26th April 1976.

South African born, yet British based, comic actor Sid James was a much loved and intrinsic part of British comedy for almost 30 years. He is most famously remembered for predominantly three things: his role as Tony Hancock's co-star in Hancock's Half Hour, his numerous roles as part of the 'Carry On' films' team, and last but not least, his extraordinarily distinctive dirty laugh!

Whilst still living in South Africa, James had turned to acting and joined the Johannesburg Repertory Players, which then led to him working for the South African Broadcasting Corporation. During World War II he served as a lieutenant in an entertainment unit of the South African Army.

James moved to the U.K. in 1946 and it only took a year before his talent was spotted and his British acting career began. This is said because his debut appearances on screen were in the 1947 crime dramas, Night Beat and Black Memory.

Comedy came a few years later when, in 1951, he was cast in his first comedy role The Lavender Hill Mob, in which he played alongside Alfie Bass, Alec Guinness and Stanley Holloway. It was a good year for James and he was also cast in The Galloping Major and Lady Godiva Rides Again.

James was doing remarkably well considering how many years he had been on the scene. The role and character that really cemented his place in the hearts and minds of the great British public was, however, as Sid 'Balmoral' James, with Tony Hancock on BBC radio's Hancock's Half Hour. As soon as the television series was broadcast alternately with the radio show, James' part in proceedings was greatly increased. In fact, some viewed Hancock and James as a comedy double act, much to the annoyance of Hancock it later turned out.

The second aspect of James' career that enhanced his standing as a household favourite was when he became a leading member of the 'Carry On' films' team. He was part of the crew for 19 of the films in total, which made him one of the most regularly featured actors of the entire cast.

In addition to his film roles, James was also doing very nicely in the television sitcom world. His leading roles in this field of entertainment included Citizen James, Taxi!, George and the Dragon, Two in Clover, and Bless This House.

Once described by Bruce Forsyth as 'a natural at being a natural', James had a heart attack on stage at the Sunderland Empire Theatre during a production of Irish playwright Sam Cree's The Mating Game in April 1976.

Highlights:
Open All Hours
Only Fools and Horses
The Darling Buds of May

Awards:
OBE
Knighthood
Four BAFTAs
Four British Comedy Awards
Six National Television Awards

LEFT Sid James and Barbara Windsor in the famous Carry on Camping bikini scene

David Jason

Sir David Jason, OBE was born David John White on 2nd February 1940 in Edmonton, London.

O ne of our nation's favourite television character actors, David Jason is one of our rare talents whose popularity crosses generation boundaries of television audiences. As a multi-award winning actor, Jason has proven himself as both a comic and serious actor throughout his career.

Jason's rise to stardom began in 1964 when he played Bert Bradshaw in the soap opera Crossroads. He was cast as Captain Fantastic in the comedy-sketch series Do Not Adjust Your Set, which ran from 1967 to 1969. In The Top Secret Life of Edgar Briggs in 1974, Jason was cast as the accident-prone undercover man. In the much loved British sitcom Open All Hours, he played the part of the hapless shop assistant Granville in the first series broadcast in 1976. By the middle of the 1970s Jason had already firmly established himself as a regular and highly adaptable television comedy actor.

The award winning BBC sitcom Only Fools and Horses, created and written by John Sullivan, was originally broadcast between 1981 and 1991 plus Christmas specials. Jason as Derek Trotter, 'Del Boy', was quite literally the star of the show. This was the role that turned Jason from a known and popular actor in the eyes of the British audience, to a comedy star and enduring legend; Derek Trotter and his 'Del Boyisms' infiltrated lives, and still do! Only Fools and Horses was voted as Britain's Best Sitcom in a BBC poll carried out in 2004.

Cast as Pop Larkin in the BBC comedy drama The Darling Buds of May, which ran from 1991 to 1993, Jason made the difficult move away from his wheeler-dealer, everything's 'alwight' image. But has he ever managed to shake off his alter ego?

From 1992 to 2010 Jason then took on a more serious character role as Detective Inspector Jack Frost in the crime drama A Touch of Frost. The problem is that the hilarious 'Del Boy' character has always stuck with him. Arguably it is not so easy to see him in a serious role. That doesn't mean that he is not a totally accomplished and talented straight actor, quite the contrary. It is just that one is always waiting for a side-splitting one-liner to pop out at any moment!

In a nutshell, Jason has played numerous characters through which he has captivated British audiences for many years. His ability to bring these characters to life in such a way that they seem real, like they are part of the family, is a testament to his acting and performance skills.

For services to acting and comedy, Jason was awarded an OBE in 1993 before being knighted in 2005. He has won four BAFTAs, four British Comedy Awards and six National Television Awards.

Highlights:
Open All Hours
**Only Fools
and Horses**
**The Darling
Buds of May**

Awards:
OBE
Knighthood
Four BAFTAs
**Four British
Comedy Awards**
**Six National
Television Awards**

LEFT Del Boy and Rodney from Only Fools and Horses

Peter Kay

Peter John Kay was born on 2nd July 1973 in Bolton, Greater Manchester.

One of Britain's most recent comedy phenomena, award winning stand-up comedian Peter Kay has risen to stardom and already become a household name, and his career only began in 1996. He is an all round show business talent and has added writing, acting, directing and producing skills to his comedy bow.

Even as a child Kay was hooked on making people laugh, but his big career break came in 1996 when he won the North West Comedian of the Year competition. Kay hadn't in fact done much stand-up comedy prior to this competition, but following this success his rise in fame and popularity was simply meteoric.

Kay's home town of Bolton remains very dear to him and his life and experiences there form the basis of much of his stand-up comedy material. His humour is observational and clean, easy-going and honest, with very little obscenities or adult-only content.

Branching out into television comedy Kay wrote, directed, and starred in a series of six spoof documentaries, That Peter Kay Thing in 2000. This was followed by the BAFTA-winning sitcom Phoenix Nights the following year, and the comedy television show Max and Paddy's Road to Nowhere in 2004.

Other and quite diverse screen work in Kay's career to date has included: Coronation Street, Dr. Who, and Wallace and Gromit: The Curse of the Were-Rabbit, to name a few.

Kay's self-penned autobiography The Sound of Laughter, published in 2006, has become one of the best

Highlights:
**Peter Kay Thing
Phoenix Nights
Max and Paddy's
Road to Nowhere
Amarillo**

Awards:
**Four British
Comedy Awards
Four Royal
Television Society
Awards
The Rose D'Or
in Montreux at
the International
Television Festival
AFTA/LA Award**

selling British autobiographies of all time; in the first three months of publication it sold over one million copies. The recording of his Mum Wants a Bungalow tour also holds the record for being the biggest selling British stand-up DVD.

Not complete without adding a hit single to his remarkable career so far, Kay's Comic Relief video in 2005 led to the song (Is This The Way to) Amarillo?

sitting at number one in the charts for seven weeks. It raised over two million pounds for Comic Relief.

Since his first career-launching comedy win, Kay has since won four British Comedy Awards (including writer of the year), four Royal Television Society Awards, the Rose D'Or in Montreux at the International Television Festival, and a BAFTA/LA Award for the 2009 Britain's Got The Pop Factor.

Stan Laurel

Stan Laurel was born **Arthur Stanley Jefferson** on 16th June 1890 in Ulverston, Lancashire, and died at the age of 74 on 23rd February 1965.

RIGHT Stan Laurel on the left with his comedy partner Oliver Hardy

As the slimmer half of the comedy duo Laurel & Hardy, the English comic Stan Laurel was one of the great heavyweights of cinematic comedy.

In a film acting career that stretched from 1917 to 1951, it included a starring role in the Academy Award winning film The Music Box in 1932. He became an international star as the equally incompetent sidekick to the know-all Oliver Hardy. Their comedy was pure slapstick though never malicious, and their affection for each other shone through the mayhem.

Born Arthur Stanley Jefferson at Ulverston in Lancashire, his parents were both active in the theatre and he made his first professional appearance at Glasgow's Metropole Theatre, which was managed by his father.

In 1910, with the stage name of Stan Jefferson, he joined Fred Karno's troupe of actors (which also included a young Charlie Chaplin) and they toured America where he worked briefly alongside Oliver Hardy in a silent film, The Lucky Dog, before the two were a team.

It was around this time that Stan met actress Mae Dahlberg who persuaded him to adopt the stage surname of 'Laurel' and they worked on several films together before she went back to her native Australia.

Laurel went on to join the Hal Roach studio, intending to work primarily as a writer and director, before fate stepped in when Hardy was injured in a kitchen mishap and Laurel was asked to return to acting.

They began sharing the screen in Slipping Wives, Duck Soup and With Love and Hisses, and their comic chemistry soon became obvious. Roach Studios' supervising director Leo McCarey noticed the audience reaction to them, leading to the creation of the Laurel and Hardy series.

Together, the two men began producing a huge body of short films, including The Battle of the Century, Should Married Men Go Home?, Two Tars, Be Big!, Big Business, and many others. Laurel and Hardy successfully made the transition to talking films with the short Unaccustomed As We Are in 1929.

During the 1930s, Laurel was involved in a legal dispute with Hal Roach, and didn't star alongside Hardy for a number of years until they made A Chump at Oxford and subsequently, Saps at Sea, which was their last film for Roach.

In 1939, Laurel and Hardy signed a contract at 20th Century Fox and for the next years their work became more standardised and less successful, though The Bullfighters, Great Guns and A-Haunting We Will Go did receive some praise.

In 1950, Laurel and Hardy were invited to France to make a feature film, a French-Italian co-production titled Atoll K, which was a disaster. (The film was titled Utopia in the U.S. and Robinson Crusoeland in the U.K.) Both stars were noticeably ill during the filming and upon returning home, spent most of their time recovering.

Never blessed with robust health, Oliver Hardy died of a heart attack in August 1957. Laurel was too ill to attend his funeral, stating, 'Babe would understand'. People who knew Laurel said he was devastated by Hardy's death and never fully recovered from it, refusing to perform ever again after his partner's death.

In 1961, Stan Laurel was given a Lifetime Achievement Academy Award for his pioneering work in comedy. He had achieved his lifelong dream as a comedian and had been involved in nearly 190 films.

He died in February 1965, aged 74, and couldn't resist carrying on his comic routine to the very last. Just minutes away from death, Laurel told his nurse he would not mind going skiing at that very moment. Somewhat taken aback, the nurse replied that she was not aware that he was a skier. 'I'm not' said Laurel, 'I'd rather be doing that than this!'

At his funeral, silent screen comedian Buster Keaton was overheard giving his assessment of the comedian's considerable talent: 'Chaplin wasn't the funniest, I wasn't the funniest, this man was the funniest'.

Highlights:
The Music Box
The Battle of
the Century
Should Married
Men Go Home?
Big Business
A-Haunting We
Will Go

Awards:
Stan Laurel was
given a Lifetime
Achievement
Academy Award

Little and *Large*

Syd Little was born **Cyril Mead** on 19th December 1942 in Blackpool, Lancashire.

Eddie Large was born **Edward Hugh McGinnis** on 25th June 1941 in Glasgow.

The popular British comedy double act Little and Large, Syd Little and Eddie Large, were particularly popular during the 1980s with their long-running television show The Little and Large Show.

The comic duo got together in 1962 and started performing in local pubs in the northwest of England. In fact only one element of the pair did the gags, Large, whilst Little was the more serious one. Their comedy act revolved around Little trying to perform seriously, with Large constantly interrupting his jokes or impressions with insults and the like.

The pair turned professional in 1963 but they didn't ever consciously plan a serious career in comedy together as a double act, it just sort of happened. In Eddie's own words, 'We never really planned to be famous … we were quite happy with a couple of meat pies each – plus all the beer we could drink'.

The real turning point in their comedy careers and exposure to the nation's audiences came in 1971 when they won the television talent show, Opportunity Knocks.

Little and Large have been described in the press as 'Britain's least complicated comic duo', and although they were never particularly highly regarded by the critical press, their BBC series Little and Large became one of the nation's favourite Saturday evening entertainment programmes and attracted viewing figures of nearly 15 million. The series ran from 1978 to 1991 and was a family entertainment show that combined impressions, comic sketches and featured special guests.

"Their comedy act revolved around **Little** *trying to* **perform seriously,** *with* **Large** *constantly* **interrupting his jokes"**

In an effort to keep up with the times, Little and Large tried to add a further dimension to their act, but in the end the shift in popular taste towards the 'alternative' comedy scene meant that the pair were retired from their television show in 1991. Large described the time when he realised what changes were happening: 'I was watching The Young Ones on BBC 2 the other night … marvellous. But I can't help worrying what this sort of comedy is going to do to the rest of us. Will we all have to be more outrageous to keep up?'

Both continued to perform on stage in pantomimes such as Ian Billings' Babes in the Woods, and other theatre productions. Unlike Morecambe and Wise, however, Little and Large never quite won over the hearts and minds of the British audiences in the same way. Large was then diagnosed with a heart condition and the partnership split up completely.

Highlights:
BBC series
Little and Large
They won the
television talent
show, Opportunity
Knocks in 1971

"We never really planned to be famous … we were quite happy with a couple of meat pies each - plus all the beer we could drink"

Michael
McIntyre

Michael Hazen James McIntyre was born on 21st February 1976 in Merton, London.

Arguably Britain's most successful stand-up comedian to become a super-star in the last three years, Michael McIntyre, the new kid on the comedy block, has taken the country by storm since his first stand-up performances in 1999.

McIntyre's father was a well-known comedy script writer (Ray Cameron), so with laughter running through the family blood it should be no surprise that McIntyre left Edinburgh University after his first year to pursue a career along the same lines as his father.

Programmes such as Live at the Apollo have featured McIntyre several times, giving him nationwide exposure to British audiences. He has also performed three times at the Royal Variety Performance and is the youngest ever person to actually host the show, which he did in 2010.

It was his appearance at the 2006 Royal Variety Performance that really launched his career and made him a twenty-first-century comedy celebrity. McIntyre's stand-up material is based on observational social satire. Other British comedy greats who have had an influence on his style include Woody Allen, Billy Connolly, Lee Evans, Peter Kay, Jimmy Carr and, of course his father, Ray Cameron.

McIntyre's own BBC television series, Michael McIntyre's Comedy Roadshow, has been nominated for a BAFTA Award. The original six-episode series was first broadcast in 2009, commissioned due to the extraordinary success of Live at the Apollo. McIntyre hosts the programme and it features different

"*Fastest selling* stand-up DVD in the history of the *U.K. charts.*"

stand-up comedy venues around the U.K. and Ireland.

Naturally, due to his rise to comedy fame (not to mention the fact that he is quite obviously absolutely hilarious), McIntyre is a popular choice for inclusion on comedy panel shows. His television appearances have included: Chris Moyles' Quiz Night, Mock the Week, Have I Got News for You, Would I Lie To You?, and The Apprentice: You're Fired.

Featuring material from his first national tour, Live and Laughing was McIntyre's debut DVD. Released in 2008, it became the fastest selling ever. The following year he released Michael McIntyre: Hello Wembley, funnily enough, featuring material from his performances at Wembley Arena in London. This has sold over 1.4 million copies and holds the record for being the fastest selling stand-up DVD in the history of the U.K. charts.

In the same year, 2009, McIntyre was also awarded a British Comedy Award for the Best Live Stand-up comedian. In 2010 he then won the Best Male TV Comic Award.

Highlights:
Royal Variety Performance Michael McIntyre's Comedy Roadshow Live at the Apollo

Awards:
British Comedy Award for the Best Live Stand-up comedian 2009 Best Male TV Comic Award. 2010

"*Youngest ever person* to host the *Royal Variety Performance*"

Max Miller

Max Miller was born **Thomas Henry Sargent** on 21st November 1894 in Brighton, and died at the age of 68 on 7th May 1963.

Max Miller – the 'Cheeky Chappie' – was a British vaudeville comedian who topped variety bills from the 1930s to the 1950s. He was famous for his flamboyant suits, his wicked charm, and his risqué jokes, which often got him into trouble with the censors.

He first got the bug for entertaining when he started a troops' concert party during service in World War I, and after demobilisation he spotted an advertisement for artists to join Jack Sheppard's concert party in an alfresco theatre on Brighton beach. He applied and joined as a light comedian for the 1919 summer season. Here he met his wife Frances Kathleen Marsh, who was a contralto in the group.

The following year, they toured in a revue called The Girl and while in Plymouth they married at the parish church in Tormoham, Devon. Kathleen was an astute businesswoman and thereafter did much to develop her husband's career. She suggested that he should change his name to Max Miller.

He spent most of the 1920s touring in revues all over Great Britain and Ireland. It wasn't until February 1929, when he appointed a new agent Julius Darewski, that his career really took off.

Miller much preferred to perform solo, and from 1930 onwards he appeared in variety in various large theatres including the London Palladium and the Holborn Empire. In those days instant success was unheard of, and Miller, like any other performer, had to earn his fame through a long apprenticeship.

Whilst his timing was honed to perfection over the years, his garish stage outfit – a gloriously colourful suit with plus-fours, a kipper tie, trilby and matching shoes – would also help lighten the mood of the audience.

Although Miller's material was risqué, he never swore on stage and disapproved of those who did. He used double entendre and when telling a joke would often leave out the last word or words for the audience to complete.

When roses are red,
They're ready for plucking.
When a girl is sixteen,
She's ready for … 'Ere!

He would then say, 'I know exactly what you are saying to yourself, you're wrong, I know what you're saying. You wicked lot. You're the sort of people that get me a bad name!'

Miller appeared in three Royal Variety Performances (1931, 1937 and 1950). In the last he was angry that he only got six minutes, while the American comedian Jack Benny got 20 minutes, so he abandoned his script and went on for 12 minutes ending with riotous applause. Val Parnell, the producer, was furious and told Miller that he would never work for him again. However, after 18 months of Miller touring in secondary theatres, he was invited back to the Moss Empires, and returned in triumph to the London Palladium. This revitalised his career and with it came a new recording contract, this time with Philips. He was back on radio and appeared on television. However his television appearances were never a great success; the new medium did not suit his style.

However, Max appeared regularly in all the large variety halls in and around London, including the Hackney Empire, Chelsea Palace, Chiswick, Finsbury Park and Wood Green Empires, and the Metropolitan Music Hall. It was in the latter that he recorded the LP, Max at the Met in 1957, considered by some as his best.

Max suffered a heart attack in 1958 and after recovery needed to take life easier. His last West End appearance took place at the Palace Theatre in April 1959 and the last ever in variety at Folkestone in December 1960. He continued to make records, his last in January 1963 with Lonnie Donegan and he died at his home in Brighton in January of that year.

With dwindling work in variety, brought about by the increasing popularity of television, Max commented, 'When I'm dead and gone, the game's finished'.

Highlights:
Performed in various large theatres including the London Palladium
Three Royal Variety Performances
Radio and TV

Spike Milligan

Author, musician, poet, playwright and actor, Milligan was all these, but it was as the creative genius behind The Goon Show that he reached his comic peak.

Along with Peter Sellers and straight man Harry Secombe, they created an anarchic range of comic characters – Bluebottle, Eccles, Count Moriarty, Major Bloodnok, Henry Crun and Minnie Bannister – that are still revered as amongst the funniest in the history of radio comedy.

Milligan was born and spent his childhood in India where his Irish-born father was serving in the British Indian Army. The family came back to England and he was an accomplished jazz trumpeter before being called up for military service.

He started writing and performing comedy sketches to entertain the troops and he would compose surreal stories, filled with puns and skewed logic, as a way of staving off the boredom of life in the barracks.

He was wounded in action in Italy and after his hospitalisation, he became a full-time entertainer playing the guitar with a jazz and comedy group called The Bill Hall Trio in concert parties for the troops.

After being demobilised, Milligan returned to England and made a precarious living as a jazz musician with the Hall trio and other musical comedy acts. He was also trying to break into the world of radio, as either a performer or

Terence Alan Patrick Seán Milligan, KBE was born on 16th April 1918 in India, and died at the age of 83 on 27th February 2002.

as a script writer, and he eventually got a chance to write for comedian Derek Roy's show.

He joined forces with Peter Sellers, Harry Secombe and Michael Bentine to create a radical comedy series entitled The Goon Show. During its first sea-

co-wrote with various collaborators most notably Larry Stephens and Eric Sykes. The demands of writing and performing the series took a heavy toll, however, and he suffered several serious mental breakdowns, which also marked the onset of a decade-long cycle of

> *"Author, musician, poet, playwright and actor, Milligan was all these"*

son the BBC insisted that it was called Crazy People in an attempt to make the programme palatable to BBC officials by connecting it with the theatrical comedians The Crazy Gang.

The first episode was broadcast on 28th May 1951 on the BBC Home Service. Although he did not perform as much in the early shows Milligan eventually became a lead performer in almost all of The Goon Show episodes.

He was also the primary author of most of the scripts, although he often

manic-depressive illness.

The 15-minute series' The Telegoons was an attempt to transplant The Goons to television, this time using puppet versions of the familiar characters. The initial intention was to 'visualise' original recordings of 1950s Goon Show episodes, but this proved difficult to achieve in practice. Adaptations of the original scripts were used instead, with Milligan, Sellers and Secombe reuniting to provide the voices. Two series were made in 1963 and 1964.

Highlights:
The Hall trio
The Goon Show
The Bed-Sitting Room
Son of Oblomov

Awards:
MBE

In early 1969 Milligan starred in the ill-fated situation comedy Curry & Chips, created and written by Johnny Speight and featuring Milligan's old friend and colleague Eric Sykes. Curry & Chips set out to satirise racist attitudes in Britain in a similar vein to Speight's earlier creation, the hugely successful Till Death Us Do Part. The series generated numerous complaints because of its frequent use of racist epithets and 'bad language' and it was cancelled on the orders of the Independent Broadcasting Authority after only six episodes.

Milligan also wrote verse, considered to be within the genre of literary nonsense. His poetry has been described by comedian Stephen Fry as 'absolutely immortal – greatly in the tradition of Lear'. His most famous poem, 'On the Ning Nang Nong', was voted the U.K.'s favourite comic poem in 1998 in a nationwide poll.

Bernard Miles gave Milligan his first straight acting role, as Ben Gunn, in the Mermaid Theatre production of Treasure Island. Miles described Milligan as … 'a man of quite extraordinary talents...a visionary who is out there alone, denied the usual contacts simply because he is so different he can't always communicate with his own species ...'.

Treasure Island played twice daily through the winter of 1961-62, and was an annual production at the Mermaid Theatre for some years. During the long pauses between the matinee and the evening show, Milligan began talking to Miles about the idea he and John Antrobus were exploring of a dramatised post-nuclear world. This became the one-act play The Bed-Sitting Room, which Milligan co-wrote with John Antrobus, and which premiered in 1962. It was adapted to a longer play, and staged by Miles at London's Mermaid Theatre, making its debut in 1963. It was a critical and commercial success, and was revived in 1967 with a provincial tour before opening at London's Saville Theatre in 1967. Finally it was made into a film in 1969.

In 1964, Milligan appeared in Frank Dunlop's production of the play Oblomov at the Lyric Theatre in London, based on the novel by Russian writer Ivan Goncharov. Per Scudamore's biography, 'Milligan's fans and the theatrical world in general found it hard to believe that he was to appear in a straight play'.

Nobody seemed at all comfortable in their roles and the audience began to hoot with laughter when Milligan's slipper inadvertently went spinning across the stage into the audience. That was the end of Spike's playing straight. When he forgot his words, or disapproved of them, he simply made it up. The following night Milligan began to ad lib in earnest. The cast were bemused, but they went along with him. Incredibly, the show began to resolve itself, but the context changed completely. Cues and lines became irrelevant as Milligan verbally rewrote the play each night. By the end of the week, Oblomov had changed beyond recognition. Following a record-breaking five week run at the Lyric Theatre, however, it was retitled Son of Oblomov and moved to the Comedy Theatre in the West End.

Even late in life, Milligan's black humour did not desert him. After the death of Harry Secombe from cancer, he said, 'I'm glad he died before me, because I didn't want him to sing at my funeral'.

Milligan died from liver disease at his home having previously quipped that he wanted his headstone to bear the words 'I told you I was ill'.

Warren
Mitchell

Warren Mitchell
was born
Warren Misell
on 14th January
1926 in Stoke
Newington,
London.

Award-winning actor Warren Mitchell is one of Britain's most treasured possessions. Totally at home on the stage, on the screen or on television, Mitchell is most certainly one of the most talented and versatile actors born in the twentieth century.

Drawn to acting from an early age, Mitchell was just seven when he attended Gladys Gordon's Academy of Dramatic Arts in Walthamstow, East London. Whilst studying at Oxford University he met actor Richard Burton and then served with him in the Royal Air Force. Burton pushed Mitchell to follow his acting instinct, and after the war he enrolled at RADA.

Mitchell turned out to be an extremely versatile actor, and whilst most men would be horrified, the fact that he went bald at such a young age opened up many more roles to him as he could therefore play characters of any age.

For such a talented actor, it took, perhaps surprisingly, a while for Mitchell to break into the world of television. But as we know, once he did, the rest was history! Appearing in four episodes of Hancock's Half Hour in 1955 as his debut, he went on to secure regular television parts. His first title role was offered to him in 1957 in ITV's Three 'Tough' Guys. Other popular programmes at the time that he appeared in included William Tell, Four Just Men, Sir Francis Drake, The Avengers, Danger Man and The Saint.

Of course the character with which Mitchell is most commonly associated is that of the shaved headed, racist, narrow-minded Alf Garnett. The character was first created in 1965 for a one-off play for the BBC's Comedy Playhouse series. From there the character grew and grew. Till Death Us Do Part ran from 1966 to 1974, and In Sickness and In Health from 1985 to 1992.

Mitchell's mastery of characterising Alf Garnett so wonderfully over the years made Garnett somewhat a national hero; perhaps slightly worrying considering what the character's core values and beliefs were! Alf Garnett was to live on, and in the late 1990s spin-offs such as An Audience with Alf Garnett and The Thoughts of Chairman Alf kept him well and truly alive for the British audience.

The testimony to Mitchell's acting talent lies in the fact that although he played the part of Cockney bigot Alf Garnett over the span of four decades, he has never been typecast forever in that role.

Mitchell has been a hugely successful actor since 1951 and has appeared in numerous television series, dramas, films and theatrical productions (most notably his performance as

Willie Loman in Arthur Miller's play Death of a Salesman, for which he received a Laurence Oliver Theatre Award). Some have been mentioned here, but these only scrape the surface with regard to the breadth and depth of his acting career, and his contribution to the entertainment industry over the years.

Highlights:
'Tough' Guys
Till Death Us
Do Part
In Sickness
and In Health
Death of a
Salesman

Awards:
Laurence Oliver
Theatre Award

Bob Monkhouse

Robert Alan Monkhouse, OBE was born on 1st June 1928 in Beckenham, Kent. He died at the age of 75 on 29th December 2003.

Known in his later life as 'King of the Game Shows' and famous for his 'one-liners', Bob Monkhouse was one of those comic entertainers that you either love or hate. Whichever camp you sit in, the fact remains that Monkhouse contributed a lifetime's commitment to the British entertainment industry, his performing career spanning 50 years.

Unlike many of his contemporaries, Monkhouse missed the usual comedy apprenticeship of performing in music halls. By the time he was 19 he had successfully auditioned for BBC radio and performed on numerous shows, sometimes as the resident comedian.

Expanding his skills to comedy writing, Monkhouse met comedian and writer Denis Goodwin in 1948. Together they wrote scripts for comedians such as Arthur Askey, Jimmy Edwards, Ted Ray and Max Miller. In addition to writing for numerous BBC radio shows, the pair also performed as a double act.

Naturally, the success of their radio shows led to the genre of television. The first of their own shows was the sketch series Fast and Loose that ran from 1954 to 1955. Other joint ventures included the sitcom My Pal Bob that ran from 1957 to 1958, and The Bob Monkhouse Hour, a series of five comedy specials that were broadcast over the following two years. Not such a success was the 1964 sitcom The Big Noise. Despite their titles, all of these were co-written and performed by Goodwin as well as Monkhouse. Monkhouse was the name, however, that was perceived as the 'star' half of the duo.

Monkhouse had also kept his solo career running simultaneously alongside his work with Goodwin. He hosted Val Parnell's Sunday Night at the

London Palladium in 1957 and Candid Camera from 1960 to 1962. During this period Monkhouse also appeared in several films including Carry On Sergeant, the very first 'Carry On' film in 1958.

Having split with Goodwin in 1965, the following years of Monkhouse's career shifted to the genre for which he is, perhaps unfortunately, most associated: the game show. He hosted nearly 30 of them throughout his career including For Love or Money, The Golden Shot, Family Fortunes, Bob's Full House, and Opportunity Knocks.

Critically, Monkhouse had quite a tough time and he was often labelled as smarmy, insincere or greasy in the press. Admittedly his style was slick, and was greatly influenced by American performers such as Bob Hope. None of this stopped Monkhouse cracking on with his career, however, and his confidence in his own ability carried him on. He knew that he was a respected stand-up comedian in his own right.

Despite his love of hosting game shows, Monkhouse did also continue his television comedy work: The Bob Monkhouse Comedy Hour in 1972 and The Bob Monkhouse Show that ran from 1983 to 1986 are good examples.

Highlights:
The Bob Monkhouse Hour
The Bob Monkhouse
Carry On Sergeant
Family Fortunes
Opportunity Knocks

Awards:
OBE

Dudley Moore

Derek and Arthur with Liza Minnelli, for which he received an Oscar nomination. He was frequently referred to in the media as 'Cuddly Dudley' or 'The Sex Thimble', a reference to his short 5' 2½" stature and reputation as a ladies' man.

Moore was born in Charing Cross Hospital, London, and was brought up in Dagenham, Essex. He was born with club feet that required extensive hospital treatment and which, coupled with his diminutive stature, made him the butt of jokes from other children. Seeking refuge from his problems, he became a choirboy at the age of six and took up piano and violin. He rapidly developed into a highly talented pianist and organist.

His musical talent won him an organ scholarship to Magdalen College, Oxford. While studying music and composition there, he performed with Alan

Dudley Stuart John Moore, CBE was born on 19th April 1935 in London, and died at the age of 66 on 27th March 2002.

Dudley Moore first came to prominence as one of the four writer-performers in the groundbreaking comedy revue Beyond the Fringe in the early 1960s. He cemented his reputation as one of greatest ever comic straight men as half of the popular television duo 'Pete & Dud' with Peter Cook.

He found international fame later in hit Hollywood films such as 10 with Bo

Bennett in the Oxford Revue. Bennett then recommended him to the producer putting together Beyond the Fringe, a comedy revue, where he would first meet Peter Cook. Beyond the Fringe was at the forefront of the 1960s satire boom and after success in Britain it transferred to the United States.

Moore had become an accomplished jazz pianist and composer and when he returned to the U.K. was offered his own music-based series on the BBC, Not Only... But Also in 1965. It was commissioned specifically as a vehicle for Moore, but when he invited Peter Cook on as a guest, their comedy partnership was so notable that it became a permanent fixture of the series.

Their sketches as two working-class men, Pete and Dud, in macs and cloth caps, commenting on politics and the arts, are to this day still considered as amongst the funniest in the history of comedy. Moore was famous for 'corpsing' – the programmes often went out live – and Cook would deliberately make him laugh in order to get an even bigger reaction from the studio audience.

The duo caused controversy in the late 1970s when, under the pseudonyms Derek and Clive, they created an album of obscene ramblings that many thought went beyond the bounds of decency. Following the last of these, Derek and Clive – Ad Nauseam, Moore made a break with Cook (whose alcoholism was affecting his work) to concentrate on his film career. He moved to Hollywood, where he appeared in Foul Play (1978) with Goldie Hawn and Chevy Chase.

The following year saw his break-out role in Blake Edwards's 10, and in 1981, Moore appeared as the lead in the comedy Arthur, an even bigger hit than 10, which also starred Liza Minnelli and Sir John Gielgud.

In addition to acting, Moore continued to work as a composer and pianist, writing scores for a number of films and giving piano concerts, which were highlighted by his popular parodies of classical favourites.

Moore was deeply affected by the death of Peter Cook in 1995, and for weeks would regularly telephone Cook's home in London just to get the telephone answering machine and hear his friend's voice.

At the age of 66, Moore passed away at his home in New Jersey after his long and bitter battle with Progressive Supranuclear Palsy.

Highlights:
Beyond the Fringe
Not Only...
But Also
Pete and Dud
Arthur
composer and
pianist

Awards:
CBE

Morecambe and *Wise*

Eric Morecambe, OBE was born **John Eric Bartholomew** on 14th May 1926 in Morecambe, Lancashire. He died at the age of 58 on 28th May 1984.

Ernie Wise, OBE was born **Ernest Wiseman** on 27th November 1925 in Bramley, West Riding of Yorkshire. He died at the age of 73 on 21st March 1999.

Described as 'the most illustrious, and the best-loved double-act that Britain has ever produced', Eric Morecambe and Ernie Wise achieved nationwide fame and are one of the most recognised and respected comedy partnerships of the twentieth century.

Known as Morecambe and Wise, or Eric and Ernie, their unique collaborations on the radio, television and big screen entertained British audiences for over 40 years. At the height of their popularity in the 1970s, the 1977 Morecambe and Wise Christmas Show attracted one of the highest viewing ratings in the history of British television, with 28 million viewers.

They first met when still teenagers in 1941, both having had some performing experience. Reunited in 1946 after the war, they began to work seriously on their double act. Their debut television performance was in 1951 on the BBC's Parade of Youth show. It was working in radio, however, that first gave them notable exposure and initiated their rise to fame.

Following the success of their contribution to the radio show Variety Fanfare in 1952, they secured their first own radio series, You're Only Young Once, which ran from 1953 to 1954.

Their radio show and simultaneous television appearances during this time led to the duo being offered their first BBC television series. In fact the series Running Wild turned out to be a disaster and their inexperience was horribly exposed.

*"Known as **Morecambe** and **Wise**, or **Eric and Ernie**, their unique collaborations on the radio, television and big screen **entertained British audiences** for over **40 years**."*

Had more people in the country owned televisions at the time it could have quite conceivably ended their careers. Luckily, however, the damage was reversible.

Determined to rectify the situation and now working with Sid Green and Dick Hills, billed as The Morecambe and Wise Show but titled on screen as Two of a Kind, the series ran from 1961 to 1968. It put the pair firmly back on the comedy chart and rising; they were swiftly becoming the nation's favourite comedy team.

Moving to the BBC in 1968 saw the blossoming of their heyday. The Morecambe and Wise Show ran from 1968 to 1977. Although Green and Hills wrote the first series, Eddie Braben took over from there and it was during this time that the duo's most loved and remembered style and catchphrases were developed. Morecambe and Wise became two of the most loved comedians British audiences had ever seen. Recurring one-liners such as 'What do you think of it so far? Rubbish!', and 'You told me it was flippin' finished', have lived on even after the death of both comedians.

Morecambe and Wise's television shows won them six BAFTA Awards between 1963 and 1977 and they were both awarded the OBE in 1976.

Highlights:
Beyond Our Ken
Dad's Army
'Carry On' films
The Magnificent Seven Deadly Sins

Awards:
Six BAFTA AWARDS
OBE's

Bill
Pertwee

**William
Desmond
Anthony
Pertwee, MBE**
was born on
21st July 1926
Buckinghamshire.

Most fondly remembered for his part as ARP Warden Hodges in the hugely popular sitcom Dad's Army, Bill Pertwee's comedy acting career spanned nearly 30 years, from 1968 to 1997. A talented and funny actor, he was at home on radio, television, and on the big screen.

Pertwee had a fairly tumultuous childhood and his education suffered as a result. His father died when he was only 12 years old, and the family moved so many times during his formative years that he was educationally pushed from pillar to post. He also lost his brother James Raymond Pertwee in 1941 following the crash of the RAF bomber that he was piloting.

Following a stint in the Royal Air Force himself, Pertwee worked as an accounts clerk and then as a salesman for the designer clothing company Burberry. His entertainment career didn't in fact begin until he was nearly 40 years old.

It began on the radio, and Pertwee's early radio appearances included the comedy series Beyond Our Ken, which ran from 1959 to 1964, and Round The Horne, which ran from 1965 to 1967. He also dipped his toe into television during this time and was sometimes used as the supporting act for television shows.

It was, however, in the BBC sitcom Dad's Army (written by Jimmy Perry and David Croft) that gave Pertwee nationwide exposure to British audiences. Playing the part of ARP Warden Hodges, the show was first broadcast in 1968 and the very popular series ran until 1977, totalling nine series and

80 episodes. Not only did the series regularly attract audiences of some 18 million viewers, but it is still broadcast all over the world today, such was its popularity and success. A radio adaptation was also aired based on the original television scripts.

Pertwee has written a book celebrating the series, published in 1998 to coincide with the programme's 30th anniversary. Dad's Army: The Making of a Television Legend, is the essential guide to this, one of British television's, most successful series. Pertwee is also the president of the Dad's Army Appreciation Society. To mark the 40th anniversary Pertwee and other members of the original cast celebrated at the Imperial War Museum.

Although he is most endearingly remembered for his role in Dad's Army, Pertwee did a considerable amount of television and film work outside of this. He was cast in two 'Carry On' films: Carry On Loving in 1970, and Carry On Girls in 1973. He also had a part in Graham Stark's British comedy film The Magnificent Seven Deadly Sins in 1971.

For his services to charity, Pertwee was awarded an MBE in the Queen's Birthday Honours list in 2007.

Highlights:
Beyond Our Ken
Dad's Army
'Carry On' films
The Magnificent Seven Deadly Sins

Awards:
MBE

"A talented and funny actor, he was at home on radio, television, and on the big screen."

Leslie Phillips

Leslie Samuel Phillips, CBE
was born on 20th April 1924 in Tottenham, North London.

A well-spoken, debonair, talented and successful British comedy and character actor, Leslie Phillips' performing career has been quite phenomenal. Appearing on the acting scene in 1934, he is still very much an active performer today, something of a feat considering he is nearly 90 years of age. His highly recognisable voice has become very much part of our everyday entertainment lives.

Despite the fact that the voice we now associate with as nothing other than Phillips' (that being stereotypically posh), in fact wasn't how he spoke as a child. He started life as a working class East End boy with a cockney accent. Aware that this would impede his career ambitions his mother wisely enrolled him at the Italia Conti Academy for elocution lessons.

Phillips was only 13 years old when he appeared in his first film at Pinewood Studios and a year later on stage in the West End. Incidentally, he is the only living actor who was there for Pinewood Studios' opening week in 1936.

During World War II, Phillips' military duties took him to the north of England from where he had to reignite his acting career once the war was over. Although he had no choice but to start with 'the murkiest rat-infested old playhouses and music halls in the north of England', it was during this time that he developed his light comic style and became renowned for his amusing impersonations of English stereotypes.

The real turning point in Phillips'

career came in 1959. Cast in a leading role as Lt. Pouter in the BBC's hit comedy series The Navy Lark, Phillips became a familiar voice on the radio to households nationwide. He played the role for the entire 244 episodes, the final being aired in 1977. Naturally, he was also cast in the film in 1959.

Phillips then became a familiar face on the screen and was cast in three of the early 'Carry On' films (Carry On famous being 'I say, Ding Dong'!

Not wishing, however, to be forever associated with a slightly lecherous, overly suave persona that many of his comedy characters had required of him, from the 1980s Phillips turned his skilful acting hand to character roles. Since then he has appeared in a multitude of television programmes and films, as well as continuing his theatrical life. The list is unsurprisingly long, but to

Highlights:
The Navy Lark
'Carry On' films
'Doctor' films
Midsomer
Murders
Harry Potter films
as the voice of the
'sorting hat'

*"His **highly recognisable voice** has become very much part of our everyday entertainment lives."*

Nurse, Carry On Teacher, and Carry On Constable). He only returned to the comedy team in 1992 for Carry On Columbus. Taking over from Dirk Bogarde, Phillips then appeared in several of the comedy 'Doctor' films during the 1960s.

It is no surprise that when you've been around the entertainment industry as long as Phillips has you are going to be associated forever with certain mannerisms and phrases, perhaps his most name a few of the most notable: later television programmes include British sitcoms Honey for Tea, The House of Windsor, and Midsomer Murders; later films include Empire of the Sun, The Jackal, Lara Croft: Tomb Raider, and three Harry Potter films as the voice of the 'sorting hat'.

In 1998 Phillips was appointed OBE, and 10 years later this honour was raised to CBE. His autobiography, Hello, was published in 2006.

Awards:
OBE and CBE

Harry Secombe

Sir Harry Donald Secombe, CBE was born on 8th September 1921 in Swansea, Wales. He died at the age of 79 on 11th April 2001.

For half a century Harry Secombe dedicated his life to entertaining British audiences. As well as being a talented comedy actor, he had the skill to move seamlessly between performance genres, including singing, having a particularly lovely tenor voice.

Secombe won the hearts and minds of the nation in a way that is only matched by very few of his comedy contemporaries and he is fondly remembered for his warmth, charm and effortless affability.

Secombe's passion for performing was evident from a young age, and when he was singing in his church choir, from the age of 12, he would also perform a sketch at social events called The Welsh Courtship.

Along with everyone else, Secombe did his time in the army during World War II and served as a Lance Bombardier in the Royal Artillery. Joining the cast of the Windmill Theatre in London in 1946 he met Michael Bentine and his performing career was under way in earnest.

The first serious career breakthrough Secombe had was when he joined the cast of the BBC Wales radio variety show Welsh Rarebit. At its height of popularity the programme attracted 12 million listeners and ran from 1948 to 1951. Secombe continued his radio work and also appeared on the BBC Light Programme's radio show Variety Bandbox, as well as the comedy show Educating Archie.

The role that Secombe is arguably most associated with from his early career is that of Neddie Seagoon in

the BBC radio comedy programme The Goon Show. Having already met Michael Bentine and Peter Sellers, together with Spike Milligan the quartet wrote the series, which ran from 1951 to 1960. The original series was called Crazy People. The show was enormously popular with British listeners.

Although he didn't have to do any other work at this time, Secombe continued to keep other strings to his talented bow going. He continued with his singing and trained under the Italian maestro Manlio di Veroli. In typical Secombe fashion, he regarded himself as a 'can belto' as opposed to a 'bel canto' tenor! With his talented and highly trained voice, Secombe appeared in many stage musicals and also went on to release an impressive list of best-selling singles and albums.

As well as appearing in films of the time such as Jet Storm and Davy, Secombe eventually had his own television show. The Harry Secombe Show was first broadcast in 1968 and ran until 1973.

Secombe became Sir Secombe in 1981 and, due to his somewhat rotund figure, humorously referred to himself as Sir Cumference! His further amusing touch on the occasion is evident in the fact that he chose 'Go On' as the motto for his coat of arms.

Secombe's health began to seriously decline from 1980; he had two strokes and was diagnosed with prostate cancer, which took his life. It is a testament to how the nation felt about him that, in addition to family and friends, Prince Charles, Prince Phillip, Princess Anne, Prince Edward and Princess Margaret attended his funeral.

LEFT Harry Secombe putting smiles on some famous faces

Highlights:
**Welsh Rarebit
The Goon Show
radio series
The Harry
Secombe Show
many stage
musicals
best-selling
singles and
albums**

Awards:
**Received a
knighthood
in 1981**

Peter
Sellers

Richard Henry Sellers was born on 8th September 1925 in Southsea, Portsmouth, and died at the age of 54 on 24th July 1980.

Perhaps best known as Chief Inspector Clouseau in The Pink Panther film series, older fans will also fondly remember Peter Sellers as the voice of Bluebottle and many other manic characters from The Goon Show radio series.

His ability to speak in different accents along with his perfect comic timing contributed to his success as a radio personality and screen actor and earned him national and international nominations and awards.

Born in Southsea, Portsmouth, he began to develop a gift for improvising dialogue while he was still at school. Sellers got his first job at a theatre in Ilfracombe when he was 15, starting as a janitor. He was steadily promoted, becoming a box office clerk, usher, assistant stage manager, and lighting operator. He was also offered some small acting parts. Working backstage gave him a chance to see serious actors at work, such as Paul Scofield.

He also became close friends with Derek Altman, and together they launched Sellers' first stage act under the name 'Altman and Sellers', where they played ukuleles, sang, and told jokes. They also both enjoyed reading detective stories by Dashiell Hammett, and were inspired to start their own detective agency. Their enterprise ended abruptly when a potential client ripped Sellers' fake moustache off!

During World War II, Sellers was a corporal in the Royal Air Force. As a distraction from the life of a non-commissioned officer, Sellers joined the Entertainments National Service

Association (ENSA) allowing him to hone his drumming and comedy skills.

During those years, Sellers and his soldier friend David Lodge, who later became a leading British actor, entertained the troops in Gang Shows, with Sellers on the drums. After his discharge and return to England in 1948, Sellers supported himself with stand-up routines in variety theatres. Sellers telephoned BBC radio producer Roy Speer, pretending to be Kenneth Horne, star of the radio show Much Binding in the Marsh, to get Speer to speak to him. Speer reportedly called Sellers a 'cheeky young sod' for this subterfuge.

As a result, Sellers was given an audition, which led to his work on Ray's a Laugh with comedian Ted Ray and subsequently to what many fans believe were his finest moments on The Goon Show with Spike Milligan, Harry Secombe and (originally) Michael Bentine. Sellers was the voice of the show's most popular character, Bluebottle, the raggedy schoolboy who was forever getting 'deaded'.

"His ability to speak in different accents along with his perfect comic timing contributed to his success"

Sellers' film success arrived with British comedies, including The Ladykillers, I'm All Right Jack and The Mouse That Roared. In his early film roles, he continued to exploit his ability to do accents and different voices, often in character parts and occasionally playing several distinct roles in a single film.

He began receiving international attention for his portrayal of an Indian doctor in The Millionairess with Sophia Loren. The film inspired the George Martin-produced novelty hit single Goodness Gracious Me and its follow-

Highlights:
Chief Inspector Clouseau in The Pink Panther film series,
The Goon Show radio series
The Millionairess

up Bangers and Mash, both featuring Sellers and Loren.

His characterisations came to the attention of director Stanley Kubrick who asked Sellers to play the lead in Dr. Strangelove or: How I Learned to Stop Worrying and Love the Bomb, as well as U.S. President Merkin Muffley and Group Captain Lionel Mandrake of the RAF.

In 1962 the sudden death of his father became life changing for Sellers, remembering his own history of heart trouble; soon after the death he decided to move from England to 'get away from it all'. He grabbed the first international film offer he received from director Blake Edwards, to star in The Pink Panther (1963).

Edwards' decision to hire Sellers was because his previous star for the part, Peter Ustinov, suddenly backed out. He recalls that because of Ustinov leaving the film, he was 'desperately unhappy and ready to kill, but as fate would have it, I got Mr. Sellers instead of Mr. Ustinov—thank God!'

Sellers was cast as the bumbling Chief Inspector Clouseau, for which Sellers would created his own unique 'Franglais' accent and add his own costume and makeup ideas for the part, including a moustache and trench coat.

Sellers described the character's personality he would portray: 'I'll play Clouseau with great dignity, because he thinks of himself as one of the world's best detectives. Even when he comes a cropper, he must pick himself up with that notion intact'.

The film was the first time Sellers played a 'slapstick' comedy role, and was followed by the sequel the following year, A Shot in the Dark, in which he featured even more prominently. He returned to the character for three more sequels from 1975 to 1978. The Trail of the Pink Panther, containing unused footage of Sellers, was released in 1982, after his death.

In 1979, Sellers played the role of Chance, a simple-minded gardener addicted to watching TV, in the black comedy Being There, considered by some critics to be the 'crowning triumph of Peter Sellers' remarkable career'.

On 25th July 1980, Sellers was

PETER SELLERS

LEFT Peter Sellers in 1967 with his wife at the time, Swedish Model Britt Ekland

scheduled to have a reunion dinner in London with Spike Milligan and Harry Secombe. On 22nd July, however, Sellers collapsed from a massive heart attack in his Dorchester Hotel room and fell into a coma. He died in a London hospital two days later.

In 1982, Sellers returned to the big screen as Inspector Clouseau in Trail of the Pink Panther, which was composed entirely of deleted scenes from his past three Panther movies, in particular The Pink Panther Strikes Again, with a new story written around them.

Joan Sims

Irene Joan Marion Sims was born on 9th May 1930 in Laindon, Essex. She died at the age of 71 on 27th June 2001.

RADA-trained British actress Joan Sims is most fondly remembered for her role as one of the most loyal members of the 'Carry On' team. Her acting career was admirably much more prolific and diverse than this, however, and she appeared in over 80 films between 1953 and 2000.

Sims began her performing career on a station platform in Laindon in the county of Essex, the town in which she was born. Her father being a stationmaster there meant that Sims could practise her performing on the station platform entertaining the train travellers as they bustled through the station.

Unsurprisingly, acting became the focus of her career at a young age, and she eventually graduated from RADA in 1950 when she was 19 years old.

In 1952 Sims made her London stage debut and she had complimentary reviews following her performance of Athene Seyler's maid in Breath of Spring in 1958, with many other stage performances under her belt in between. Later on she admitted that she did, however, prefer film work.

Starting her big screen career from 1953 in Will Any Gentleman? alongside George Cole, Sims went on to become known for her roles in the 'Doctor' films, the first of which she was as the austere nurse 'Rigor Mortis' in Doctor in the House. She amused audiences and became a fondly regarded cinema star from there on in.

Now renowned for her contribution and loyalty to the 'Carry On' films, she first starred in Carry On Nurse. Carry On Teacher, Carry On Constable, and

"Fondly remembered for her role as one of the most loyal members of the 'Carry On' team"

Carry On Regardless followed; her place in the team became firmly established. Sims appeared in 24 of the 31 films.

The success of the 'Carry On' films meant that Sims was now a respected and much loved actress in the eyes of the British audience. She carried on working in television and performed in numerous series, many of which are amongst the most popular that British television produced during the twentieth century.

Impossible to list all of her appearances here, but perhaps the roles for which she is most fondly remembered include: performing alongside Laurence Oliver and opposite Katharine Hepburn in the award-winning 1975 television film Love Among the Ruins; as Gran in the comedy series Till Death Us Do Part; starring as Annie Begley in the sitcom Farrington of the F.O.; as Mrs Wembley in the comedy series On the Up; and particularly for her role as Madge Hardcastle in As Time Goes By.

It is with great sadness that the life of such a popular and talented actress came to an end with Sims battling depression and alcoholism. She did, however, take control of her life the year before she died when she performed alongside Dame Judi Dench and Olympia Dukakis in the television film The Last of the Blonde Bombshells. Sims also completed her autobiography High Spirits before she took her final bow.

Highlights:
**London Stage performances
'Carry On' films
As Time Goes By
Love Among the Ruins
On the Up**

"She appeared in over 80 films"

Graham Stark

Graham William Stark was born on 20th January 1922 in Wallasey, Cheshire.

A British comedian, writer, actor and director, Graham Stark dedicated 60 years to the British entertainment industry and throughout his career appeared in over 70 films, with his last role played in the 1998 film The Incredible Adventures of Marco Polo at the age of 76.

Stark first became a recognised name with British audiences on BBC radio. He made his debut in Happy Go Lucky, written by Ray Galton and Alan Simpson. He then moved to other radio shows such as Ray's A Laugh and Educating Archie. He also sometimes appeared on The Goon Show as a stand-in if required.

Prior to Stark getting his very own sketch series, his television work at the time included the comedy sketch show A Show Called Fred and its successor Son of Fred, which were written by Spike Milligan and directed by Richard Lester. Stark played alongside his good friend Peter Sellers in both series. He also worked with Benny Hill during this period.

In 1964 Stark had achieved sufficient kudos and popularity to be offered his own sketch show with the BBC. The Graham Stark Show was written by Johnny Speight and many prolific comedy actors at the time appeared alongside Stark including Arthur Mullard, Deryck Guyler, Derek Nimmo, Patricia Hayes and Warren Mitchell.

Stark also appeared in several of the 'Pink Panther' comedy films, which were one of the most successful film series of the time. Based on the antics of the bumbling French police detective, Inspector Jacques Clouseau, the films are generally associated with Peter Sellers. Stark generally played a different character in each, such as the Inspector's stony-faced assistant called Hercule Lajoy in the 1964 film A Shot in the Dark.

of the original actor for the part James Beck in 1973.

Between 1939 and 1998 Stark was cast in an impressive number of films, and not unusually three or four in the same year. Whilst they cannot all be listed here, some of the most popular and

Highlights:
Appeared in over 70 films
Comedian, writer, actor and director
BBC Radio

"Graham Stark dedicated 60 years to the British entertainment industry"

Also a talented stage actor, in 1963 Stark was cast in the original stage play written by Spike Milligan and John Antrobus, The Bed-Sitting Room. He played the part of Lord Fortnum's doctor, Captain Pontius Kak. The play was both commercially successful and critically acclaimed.

Back on the radio, Stark became Private Joe Walker in the radio adaptation of Dad's Army following the death

notable not already mentioned include: Those Magnificent Men in Their Flying Machines in 1965; Alfie in 1966; Casino Royale in 1967; The Return of the Pink Panther in 1975; The Pink Panther Strikes Again in 1976; Revenge of the Pink Panther in 1978; Trail of the Pink Panther in 1982; Curse of the Pink Panther in 1983; and Superman III also in 1983.

Max Wall

Max Wall was born **Maxwell George Lorimer** on 12th March 1908 in Kennington, London, and died at the age of 82 on 21st May 1990.

Max Wall was a versatile English comedian and actor whose performing career covered music hall, theatre, films and television. Despite this vast body of work, he is still best remembered for his eccentric dance routines in which his rubbery black-stockinged legs would flail about the stage seemingly out of control.

Wall was born near the Oval cricket ground in London during a World War I air raid, and he and his elder brother Alex were saved from death by a cast iron bed frame. His younger brother Bunty and their Aunt Betty were killed by the bomb dropped from a German Zeppelin.

Max and Alex went to live with their father and his family, whilst their mother went to live with Harry Wallace, whom she had met on tour. When their father died of tuberculosis in 1920, aged 37, their mother married Harry Wallace, and they all moved to a pub in Essex.

Wall auditioned for a part with a touring theatre company, and made his stage debut at the age of 14 as Jack in Mother Goose with a travelling panto-mime company in the West Country featuring George Lacey. In 1925 he was a speciality dancer in the London Revue at the Lyceum. He became determined not to rely on his father's name, so abbreviated Maxwell to Max, and his stepfather's name Wallace, to Wall.

He is best remembered for his ludi-crously attired and hilariously strutting Professor Wallofski. This creation nota-bly influenced John Cleese, who has acknowledged Max Wall's influence on the creation of his own 'Ministry of Silly Walks' sketch for Monty Python. After appearing in many musicals and stage comedies in the 1930s, Wall's career went into decline, and he was reduced to working in obscure nightclubs. He then joined the RAF during World War II and served for three years until he was

Highlights:
**Theatre, Films
and Television
Aspects of
Max Wall
Professor
Wallofski**

of his voice. He secured television appearances and, having attracted Samuel Beckett's attention, he won parts in Waiting for Godot in 1979 and Krapp's Last Tape in 1984. In 1966 he appeared as Père Ubu in Jarry's Ubu Roi, and in 1972 he toured with Mott the Hoople on their 'Rock n' Roll Circus tour', gaining a new audience.

In the 1970s and 80s, Wall occasionally performed a one-man stage show, Aspects of Max Wall, in which he recaptured the humour of old-time music hall theatre. His last film appearance was in 1989 in the 12-minute film A Fear of Silence, a dark tale of a man who drives a stranger to a confession of murder by answering only 'yes' or 'no' to his questions; those two words, repeated, were his only dialogue.

On the afternoon of 20th May 1990, Wall fell at Simpson's Restaurant in central London, fracturing his skull. He never regained consciousness, and died early the next morning at Westminster Hospital.

invalided out in 1943.

Wall re-emerged during the 1950s when producers and directors rediscovered his comic talents, along with the expressive power of his tragic clown face and the distinctive sad falling cadences

Kenneth Williams

The charismatic and unique voice, and the remarkable flaring nostrils are the hallmarks of British comic actor and comedian Kenneth Williams, for which he will always be fondly remembered.

Kenneth Charles Williams was born on 22nd February 1926 in Islington, London. He died at the age of 62 on 15th April 1988.

Joining the Army in 1944 at the age of 18 as part of the Royal Engineers, Williams met Stanley Baxter and Peter Nichols on the stage when they all performed in the Combined Services Entertainment. He also showed a remarkable natural talent for memorising and reciting poems and other literary material.

Professionally, Williams' entertainment career took off from 1954. Following his performance of the Dauphin in Bernard Shaw's play St. Joan, he was spotted by the man (Dennis Main Wilson) who was casting Tony Hancock's new radio series Hancock's Half Hour. Williams contributed to the hugely successful radio series for five years and became well known to British audiences, particularly for his funny voices with the unmistakeable nasally, slightly whiny and camp inflections that could belong to no one else.

"Stop messing about!"

Once his role in Hancock's radio show had diminished, Williams moved on to other radio comedy programmes such as Beyond Our Ken and its sequel Round The Horne. Performing alongside Kenneth Horne the pair became well known for their comic double entendres, often with homosexual connotations.

By the time Williams was cast in his first 'Carry On' film in 1958 (Carry On Sergeant), his well-known comedy character fitted perfectly for the roles he went on to play. With 26 'Carry On' films over a 20-year period under his belt, Williams holds the record for the most performances of any member of the comedy team. He will always be remembered for certain catchphrases such as 'Stop messing about!' and 'Oh, get on with it!'

At the end of the 'Carry On' film era Williams continued with his career in television and on the radio. For example, he was a panellist on Just A Minute. In fact he contributed to BBC Radio 4's comedy programme from 1968 until his death 20 years later. In television he was a regular on What's My Line, read books on the children's series Jackanory, was the voice for the Willow the Wisp children's series, and was a guest on Michael Parkinson's chat show eight times.

Williams' autobiography, The Kenneth Williams Diaries, was published in 1993, which reignited public interest in him and he became a popular guest on the chat-show circuit following its publication. Williams was a very private person and was generally very critical of his own work. Before his death he recorded two radio documentary programmes called Carry On Kenneth, during which he spoke about his life. He revealed how his life had been hounded by loneliness and a constant sense of underachievement.

Williams died in his flat in 1988 from an overdose of barbiturates, although it was never established if it was an accident or suicide.

Highlights:
Hancock's
Half Hour
'Carry On' films
BBC Radio
4's comedy
programme

"Oh, get on with it!"

Richard
Wilson

Ian Carmichael
Wilson, OBE
was born on
9th July 1936
in Greenock,
Renfrewshire in
Scotland.

Scottish actor, broadcaster and theatre director Richard Wilson is a much loved and popular personality most well known for his character Victor Meldrew in the BBC sitcom One Foot in the Grave. His prolific career has spanned nearly half a century to date and his talent has seen him move seamlessly from the stage (as director and performer) to film and television.

Wilson's early life was quite the opposite of what it is now. He initially went into scientific research and performed his National Service with the Royal Army Medical Core. Wilson didn't in fact turn his hand to acting until he was 27 years old. He went to RADA and started developing his career from there by performing in repertory theatres in Glasgow, Edinburgh and Manchester.

For his role as Victor Meldrew in One Foot in the Grave Wilson won two Light Entertainment BAFTA Awards and the British Comedy Awards' Top Television Comedy Actor. The BBC sitcom, written by David Renwick, ran for six series in total from early 1990 to 2000. The series itself was extremely popular and won the BAFTA Award for Best Comedy in 1992.

Like so many actors who have performed a certain character so well and for so long, poor Wilson will forever be remembered for his famous phrase 'I don't believe it!'

Wilson's television career, apart from being Victor Meldrew, has been vast and varied. Impossible to list his entire contribution here, notable television work, however, includes appearances in: The Sweeney; Some Mothers Do 'Ave Em; Doctor Who; Life As We Know It; Jeffrey Archer: The Truth; and Merlin. Most recently Wilson has presented Dispatches, the Channel 4 current affairs programme called Train Journeys From Hell, and narrated Confessions from the Underground.

Work in the theatre has always played an important part of Wilson's life and he is a respected and critically acclaimed actor and theatre director. Some of his most prolific roles as an actor include: playing Malvolio in Twelfth Night with the Royal Shakespeare Company; Dr Rance in What the Butler Saw with the Royal National Theatre; and Vladimir in Waiting for Godot with the Traverse Theatre in Edinburgh and the Royal Exchange Theatre in Manchester.

As a theatrical director Wilson has put his magical touch on a diverse range of plays over the years. Notably in 2000 he won the TMA (Theatrical Management Association) Best Director Award for Mr Kolpert. Other directorial works include The Woman Before, East Coast Chicken Supper, and Rainbow Kiss.

For services to drama, as both director and actor, Wilson was awarded the OBE in 1994. Written by James Roose-Evans, One Foot on the Stage: The Biography of Richard Wilson was published in 1997.

> ❝*Wilson will forever be remembered for his famous phrase, **I don't believe it!**❞*

Highlights:
**Broadcasting & Directing
One Foot in the Grave
Twelfth Night**

Awards:
**Two BAFTA Awards
British Comedy Awards' Top Television Comedy Actor
TMA Best Director Award
OBE**

Barbara Windsor

Barbara Windsor, MBE was born **Barbara Ann Deeks** on 6th August 1937 in Shoreditch, London.

Cheeky-faced, saucy and petite Barbara Windsor became a famous and much loved comedy actress on our screens from the 1950s. A blonde bombshell with perhaps the dirtiest female giggle British audiences have ever heard, Windsor somehow escaped being labelled as a sex symbol, but became cast in a comic caricature way instead.

Windsor attended Aida Foster Stage School in Golders Green, during which time she appeared on the West End stage in the chorus line for Love From Judy when she was only 13 years old. She also worked as a film extra, and sang in West End nightclubs. With her buxom figure and cheeky smile, by the late 1950s Windsor had also become a magazine pin-up.

Stage work has always remained a big part of Windsor's acting career and she has been cast in a wide range of plays, musicals and pantomimes since her debut in the 1950s. These include: Oh! What a Lovely War in 1964; Twelfth Night in 1976; Calamity Jane in 1979;

"A *blonde bombshell* with *perhaps* the dirtiest female *giggle* British audiences have ever heard"

and numerous appearances over the years in pantomimes such as Cinderella, Aladdin, and Dick Whittington.

Her debut film appearance was in 1954 in The Belles of St. Trinian's. This led to her major career break that came in 1959 when she appeared in the East End musical Fings Ain't Wot They Used T'be. This was followed by Joan Littlewood's play and 1963 film Sparrows Can't Sing, for which Windsor was nominated as Best British Actress at the British Academy Awards.

Although Windsor is now associated with the Queen Vic in the BBC soap opera EastEnders, prior to her joining the cast, she was perhaps best known for her place in the 'Carry On' films. She appeared in nine of them in total and was often cast as the comic foil for Sid James. Arguably her most famously

remembered performance was in Carry On Camping in 1969, when her bikini top pinged off into Sid James' face.

Windsor has been cast in a variety of other films over the years, such as Too Hot to Handle in 1959, Chitty Chitty Bang Bang in 1968, and most recently the 2010 film adaptation of Alice in Wonderland.

Joining the cast of EastEnders in 1994 as Peggy Mitchell, landlady of the Queen Vic in Albert Square, Windsor earned herself a Best Actress Award at the British Soap Awards in 1999. Apart from a forced two-year absence from the soap due to illness, Windsor continued to rule her (often unruly) Mitchell family with a rod of iron until 2010.

Windsor's autobiography, All of Me: My Extraordinary Life, was published in 2000.

Highlights:
Musicals and Pantomimes
'Carry On' films
EastEnders
Alice in Wonderland

Awards:
Best Actress Award at the British Soap Awards
MBE

Mike and *Bernie* Winters

Bernie Winters was born **Bernie Weinstein** on 6th September 1932 in Islington, London. He died at the age of 58 on 4th May 1991.

Mike Winters was born **Michael Weinstein** on 15th November 1930 in Islington, London.

British comedy double act and brothers, Mike and Bernie Winters, became popular faces on television from the 1950s to the late 1970s, after which time they went their separate ways. Born into a streetwise Islington family, they were both involved in variety shows from a young age.

Their performing talents developed from a purely musical focus to dance and comedy. It was not until the early 1950s, however, that the pair saw any serious potential in pursuing a career in show business. Performing as two of the three characters with Jack Farr in the comedy act Three Loose Screws, they started making a successful name for themselves on the variety circuit.

Their television debut was in 1955 when they appeared on the BBC's Variety Parade. Between 1957 and 1958 they went on to become resident comics on the BBC's Six-Five Special. They were critically well received, with the Daily Mirror describing them as the favourite comedians for the British teenage viewers at the time.

The sibling double act worked, as many comic duos did at the time, with one (Mike) acting as the straight character and the other (Bernie) performing as the idiot, albeit a lovable one! They became renowned for phrases such as 'choochy face', and 'shut up or I'll smash your face!'

From the early 1960s the pair became a firmly established comedy duo and their popularity grew. Particularly influential to their success were two things: performing on the highly popular variety show Sunday Night at the London Palladium, followed by an invitation to perform at the 1962 Royal Variety Show. They also became resident comics and then compères on ITV's Big Night Out and then Blackpool Night.

Their hard work paid off and they were offered their own television show. Starting as Mike and Bernie's Scene, the title changed to Mike and Bernie's Special Variety Show and finally to simply Mike and Bernie Winters.

The brothers performed together until 1978, but with ever-growing tensions between them they split up for good and never performed together again. Mike went to the U.S. and Bernie continued a solo entertainment career in the U.K. One of his most fondly remembered series was with his canine partner, Schnorbitz the St. Bernard.

Bernie went on to present several television shows including, The Big Top Variety Show, a television series of variety performances that was held in a circus ring during the late 1970s and early 1980s. He also presented the second series of the game show called Whose Baby? in 1984 and a quiz show called Scribble in 1987.

Highlights:
Three Loose Screws
BBC's Six-Five Special
Sunday Night at the London Palladium
Mike and Bernie's Scene

Norman Wisdom

Sir Norman Joseph Wisdom, OBE was born on 4th February 1915 in Marylebone, London. He died at the age of 95 on 4th October 2010.

One of our most loved and respected post-war comedians; Norman Wisdom achieved international fame as a comic actor, and was also a talented singer-songwriter. Described by Charlie Chaplin as his 'favourite clown', Wisdom dedicated 60 years of his life to the world of show business and received an OBE in 1995, followed by his knighthood in 2000. He only retired from acting due to his declining health and was 90 years of age when he died.

Wisdom's show business career didn't begin until he was 31 years old. Having left the Army in 1946 he made his debut as an entertainer. His trademark looks that he will always be associated with (skew-whiff flat cap, crumpled collar and messy tie, wearing a suit far too small) were already in place as the 'Gump' character that made his film career.

In fact Wisdom's rise to fame was unusually and exponentially fast. Within two years of his debut appearance he was a recognised name on the West End stage, swiftly followed by his television debut. It did not take long for him to have a substantial British audience following.

The series of low-budget comedy films that were produced by Rank Organisation between 1953 and 1966 made Wisdom a national and international celebrity. Playing the hapless Gump character Norman Pitkin, the first film Trouble in Store earned him a BAFTA Award for Most Promising Newcomer to Film. Although these films were never particularly highly regarded by critics, British and some audiences overseas thought differently. The films were up there with the biggest British box office ratings of the day, and by 1960 Wisdom was still the tenth most popular British big screen star.

Wisdom then left the U.K. for the U.S. in 1966 and starred in a Broadway production of Walking Happy, a musical comedy written by James Van Heusen and Sammy Cahn. He was nominated for a Tony Award for his performance.

The latter half of his career saw its ups and downs as his popularity came and went with changing vogues. He continued to do his stage performances and sang his theme song Don't Laugh At Me for Queen Elizabeth II's Silver Jubilee on the BBC's A Jubilee of Music. In fact, during his career he performed in front of her numerous times. He toured the world with his cabaret act and also carried on with television work.

The emergence of young comedian Lee Evans meant that Wisdom saw resurgence in popularity in the 1990s. Evans' work, quite obviously heavily influenced by Wisdom, meant that his classic films were repeated and he found new fans of a different generation.

Having officially retired in 2005, Wisdom returned for one final film in 2007. Directed by Kevin Powis, Expresso was premiered at the Cannes Film Festival. Wisdom's health was sadly deteriorating by this time and

with the release of the film also came the news that he was suffering from vascular dementia and was being cared for in a nursing home.

Highlights:
Performed around the world
Rank Organisation Films
Broadway production of Walking Happy

Awards:
OBE & Knighthood
BAFTA Award

Victoria Wood

**Victoria Wood,
CBE** was born on
19th May 1953
in Prestwich,
Lancashire.

Now one of Britain's most popular and successful stand-up comedians, comedienne, screenwriter, director, actress and singer-songwriter Victoria Wood has become a multi-award winning and celebrated comedy star over the past 30 years. Famous for her observational and often satirical humour, Wood's material is drawn from everyday life. As a talented writer she has even been compared to the master of understated social commentary, Alan Bennett.

Whilst still at University studying drama, Wood's entertainment career got under way when she appeared and won the television talent show New Faces in 1974. Between then and 1978 Wood began to make a name for herself and appeared in various shows includ-

ing That's Life! in 1976 and the theatre revue In At The Death in 1978. Not only did she perform with her long-term collaborator-to-be Julie Walters, the show's success led to Wood's first commissioned play, Talent. In addition to this work winning her the Most Promising New Writer, spotted by the head of drama at Granada Television (Peter Eckersley), Wood was invited to create a television adaptation of it.

Two further plays for Granada followed, Nearly a Happy Ending and Happy Since I Met You, both successful Wood and Walters collaborations. A show of their own swiftly followed on New Year's Day in 1981, which led to a seven-part series, Wood and Walters, the following year.

The support and breaks that Eckersley had created for Wood came to an end when he died and in 1985 she moved to the BBC. The result, Victoria Wood – As Seen on TV, was the final comedy-career building block Wood required.

Wood had established a formidable, loyal and talented team around her that included Celia Imrie, Duncan Preston and, of course, Julie Walters. This team, with the addition of Ann Reid and others, formed the repertory company for much of Wood's following work, her BBC series Victoria Wood in 1989 as a good example.

Having had great success with the ambitious feature length drama Pat and Margaret in 1994, Woods went on to write, co-produce and star in her first and only sitcom to date, dinnerladies. The two series ran from 1998 to 2000, for which Wood won the British Comedy Award for Writer of the Year. A serious drama for ITV followed in 2006. Housewife, 49 received great reviews and Wood won BAFTA Awards for her writing and acting.

Wood's career and kudos has gone from strength to strength. Her talent to create rich and complex characters, alongside her skill for understanding language, is key to her identity. With the calibre of people she works with her future as a celebrated British comedian and writer looks very rosy indeed.

Wood's career achievements to date include five BAFTA Awards and five British Comedy Awards. She was appointed OBE in 1997 and then CBE in the 2008 Queen's Birthday Honours list.

Highlights:
**Stand up
perfomances
Writing &
Directing
Victoria Wood –
As Seen on TV
Victoria Wood
Series
Dinnerladies**

Awards:
**Five BAFTA
Awards
Five British
Comedy Awards
OBE & CBE**

ERIC SYKES
4th May 1923 – 4th July 2012

The multi-talented Eric Sykes whose career as a radio, television and film writer and actor may not have spanned the heights of the some of the household names in this book but without doubt he was one of the best-loved comic talents this country has ever produced. He first came to prominence through his many radio credits as a writer and actor in the 1950s most notably through his collaboration on The Goon Show scripts with Spike Milligan. He became a television star in his own right in the early 1960s when he appeared with Hattie Jacques in several popular sitcoms which he also wrote. One of his best remembered films is the slapstick wordless comedy The Plank while his other unusual claim to fame was that he provided narration for the Teletubbies and was featured on a number one single in December 1997 – not many in this book can make such a claim!

"...adorable, brilliant, modest, hilarious, innovative and irreplaceable comic master" Stephen Fry

Illustrated by:

JOHN IRELAND

Design & Artwork: ALEX YOUNG

Published by: DEMAND MEDIA LIMITED & G2 ENTERTAINMENT LIMITED

Publishers: JASON FENWICK & JULES GAMMOND

Written by: MICHELLE BRACHET